MAKING WAVES

The modern art statue at the front of the Vasco da Gama Shopping Center in Expo 98 Park (Parque das Nações) Lisbon.

Making Waves

The Continuing
Portuguese Adventure

Mary Soderstrom

Véhicule Press

Published with the generous assistance of The Canada Council for
the Arts, the Canada Book Fund of the Department of Canadian Heritage
and the Société de développement des entreprises culturelles du Québec
(SODEC).

Cover design: David Drummond
Set in Adobe Minion by Simon Garamond

Printed by Marquis Book Printing Inc.

LIBRARY AND ARCHIVES CANADA CATALOGUING IN PUBLICATION

Soderstrom, Mary, 1942-
Making waves : the Portuguese adventure / Mary Soderstrom.

Includes index.
ISBN 978-1-55065-292-5

1. Portugal—History. 2. Civilization, Modern—Portuguese
influences. 3. Civilization, Western—Portuguese influences.
I. Title.

DP517.S64 2010   946.9   C2010-905333-8

Published by Véhicule Press, Montréal, Québec, Canada
www.vehiculepress.com

Distribution in Canada by LitDistCo
orders@litdistco.ca

Distribution in U.S. by Independent Publishers Group
www.ipgbook.com

Printed in Canada on 100% post-consumer recycled paper.

Contents

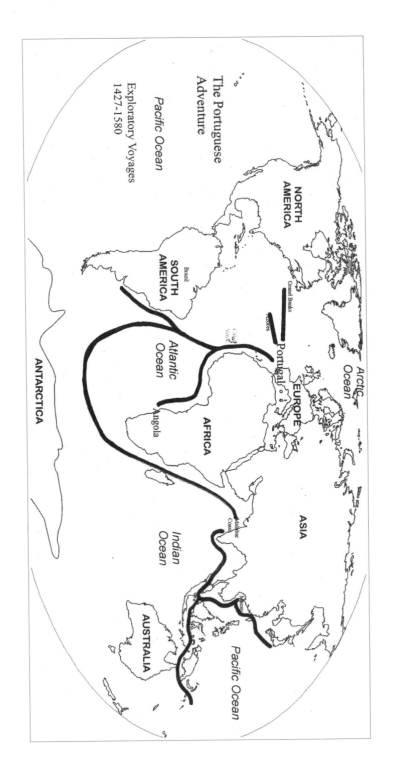

The Portuguese
Adventure

Pacific Ocean

Exploratory Voyages
1427-1580

NORTH
AMERICA

SOUTH
AMERICA

Brazil

Grand Banks

Azores

Cape
Verde

Portugal

EUROPE

Arctic
Ocean

Atlantic
Ocean

Angola

AFRICA

ASIA

ANTARCTICA

Malabar
Coast

Indian
Ocean

AUSTRALIA

Pacific Ocean

Why This Book?

LET ME ANSWER the obvious question: why does someone named Soderstrom (and born McGowan) write a book about the Portuguese? A book about the Scots or the Swedes might seem a more obvious choice. But I grew up in a landscape far more like Portugal than the Highlands of Scotland or Scandinavian fjords, so when I finally saw Portugal, I understood it immediately: the winter rains, the summer sun, the sea.

This small country with its back to Europe has made waves all out of proportion to its size for more than six hundred years: the how and why make a fascinating story.

Old Mr. Fernandes is also partly to blame. He was a fixture in my childhood in San Diego. He would pass our house early in the morning in his three-wheeled electric car, a cigar in his mouth and a fisherman's cap on his head. He always had a scarf around his neck, and a wave for my father, who was amused by the old man's punctuality.

Old man! He must have been in his seventies then, retired from fishing tuna with the San Diego fleet. He would live another twenty years, working almost until his death at ninety-three in the grocery store which his older son, Raul Jr., had started with his wife shortly after World War II.

Their store was a window on a world about which I only had a foggy idea. Everything around me was new; our house was less than ten years old, our blue Mercury sedan was wonder of sleek modernity, our new television brought us entertainment that delighted me and my sister and enthralled our parents. The people who lived on our street were all young, with young families, with great optimism and dreams that were now going to be realized after the hardships of the Great Depression and World War Two.

There were no old people among us, except for Mr. Fernandes.

Many of the neighbors had grandparents back East with interesting stories about other countries. Some of the men had seen Europe or the Far East in the War, and a block over, Mrs. Moran, we all knew, was a German war bride which was the reason why she spoke English with an accent. But if these things were talked about in the presence of children, we weren't listening. The present, this wonderful life on the far western edge of the North American continent, this place where the sun shone 300 days a year, where it snowed once a generation—that was what took all our attention.

The Fernandes store was also new. Raul Jr. and Wanda (whom he'd met at a USO dance in Louisiana after he returned from flying fifty-seven missions in World War Two in Europe) had begun with an army surplus truck they fitted out to be a traveling grocery store. The neighborhood was growing fast, but grocery shopping was a problem since neither services nor cars were readily available. Their first clients were the several hundred families of Portuguese origin who lived not far from the slips where the tuna fleet tied up at the base of Point Loma, the promontory which guards San Diego Bay. I went to school with their children, my graduating class of 500 or so at Point Loma High School included about two dozen Portuguese kids.

It took Raul Jr. and Wanda a few years to save enough to buy a lot a kilometer away from our house, in the rapidly-growing community on the peninsula. They built their store, and brought in Mr. Fernandes and Raul's brother Bob as partners.

It wasn't a big supermarket. There were a few of those around, with freezer display cabinets a small child could get lost in, pyramids of oranges and apples, and rows of breakfast cereal boxes. But my mother, who didn't have a car at her disposal, didn't shop in them. If she walked down to Raul's and made her order before noon, he would deliver it when he went home for lunch in the early afternoon. He, his wife and their three sons lived in the next block, after all. "Be glad to do it, Mrs. McGowan," he'd say at the beginning; "Sure thing, Ella" he'd say when she became a regular customer.

The attraction for me, however, was the way you could see where things came from. There would be the usual products—Tide laundry detergent, Prell shampoo, and boxes of Kleenex. But there also were cans of tomatoes and olives from Portugal, stalks of dill for making pickles, saffron, lamb carcasses that Bob would cut into legs and shanks and chops, sardines, perfect tomatoes, zucchini before they became common, little cellophane sacks containing whole black pepper, cinnamon bark, bay leaves and other dried herbs, garlic cloves, tuna canned down on the San Diego waterfront but fished off Mexico, round red globes of onions, dates from the Middle East, and occasionally strange, flat white things that Raul Jr. said were dried codfish.

It seemed amazing to me that the world was organized so that so many things from so many places could be waiting for us to buy them three blocks away from our house. It awakened my sense that the world was much bigger than our corner of it, no matter how wonderful my parents seemed to think it was where we lived. I began to hope that at some point I might see the rest of creation.

And indeed, when I grew up and married, my husband and I moved to quite a different climate—the snowy, cold winters and hot humid summers of Montreal. To my surprise, I discovered that by the late 1960s thousands of people from Portugal had also moved to Montreal for reasons with which I sympathized because they resonated with our own decision to come to Canada: They came to find better jobs, to escape politics, to avoid an incredibly stupid and draining war, and in our own way, so did we.

When the Portuguese overthrew four decades of dictatorship practically without bloodshed in 1974, I nodded: that's the way you should effect a regime change. The social transformation that followed reminded me of what had began about ten years earlier in Quebec, the place I had begun to call home by then; a society threw open its doors to reforms in education, health care, and social services. Here it was called the Quiet Revolution; there it was called the *Revolução dos Cravos*, the Carnation Revolution. Both were transformations that surprised outsiders and greatly pleased most citizens. It was as if both *le pays* that Gilles Vigneault called winter, and *o país* on the edge of Europe had been locked in ice that suddenly melted, ushering in a springtime where wildflowers of hope blossomed extravagantly. Marvelous, I thought.

Much later, two things happened which pushed me toward this project. About ten years ago I ventured away from North America for the first time. In 2000, the Conseil des arts et des lettres du Québec awarded me a grant to work on a novel, *The Violets of Usambara*. In the story is a Portuguese immigrant family from the Azorean island of São Miguel. Another family in the novel includes a Franco-American who fled the Vietnam War and who for various reasons finds himself on a fact-finding mission in the African Great Lakes region—even then the parallels between American draft dodgers and Portuguese fleeing the African wars fascinated me. I used part of the grant to go to the Azores and then to Burundi and Tanzania. As soon as I got off the airplane in São Miguel I felt at home because the landscape was so much like the Southern California I knew as a child. Later that year I was astonished to find just how many traces the Portuguese had left along the East coast of Africa.

Similar surprises awaited me over the next few years as I researched my non-fiction books. I explored botanical gardens, the relationship between people and nature in cities, and the complex problems of the way we organize our cities. I discovered that the Portuguese were the first Europeans through the Strait of Malacca which Singapore now guards. The Portuguese Vasco da Gama died on the west coast of India. Paris was home to hundreds of thousands of Portuguese emigrants. Azoreans had settled in Hawaii to fish and work on sugar plantations. They settled the vast country of Brazil.

São Paulo was one of the cities whose complicated relationship with nature I studied, and that was where my second realization about the Portuguese occurred. Not only had they traveled the world, but somehow in Brazil the descendants of the Portuguese had built a vibrant, multiracial society which, on the surface at least, appeared to be without the discriminatory barriers found in North America, particularly in the United States. Slavery had lasted longer in Brazil than in the rest of the Europeanized world, yet today São Paulo is full of confident people whose faces reflect centuries of racial mixing. How did that happen, I wondered? Is there something the rest of the world can learn here?

The journey of discovery this book proposes begins in the middle of the Atlantic on the island of Santa Maria in the Azores, where Columbus called on his way back from the New World in 1492, and where there already had been a colony in the middle of the Atlantic for more than fifty years. Then the story continues with the decades of exploration, the slave trade, the colonization of Brazil, the role of women, the Carnation Revolution, and the future of the Portuguese language. There also will be a detailed look at the reconstruction of Lisbon and the establishment of Brasília—both tell us a great deal about how people live and the role of leaders in shaping a people's destiny.

While the basic schema is chronological the story will jump around a bit, just as the Portuguese did. The book will end with reflections on what the Portuguese can teach the rest of us, as well as some musing on the amazing way paths of two similar entities can diverge. What this has to say about the way we organize our lives and our politics is a rich field for consideration.

A word about names. At the end of this book there is a timeline of major events from the eleventh century onward in Portugal as well as in places where Portuguese explorers and adventurers traveled and where Portuguese colonists settled. The names of major figures are given in full in the chronology. However, in the text the reader may find that I'm rather vague about who was who. This is because the Portuguese royal family and its outliers use the same names over and over again. Better to put my republican prejudices front and center from the beginning, and to avoid an overdose of royal names. I use the Portuguese forms of names almost exclusively. Partly this is to avoid confusion with English and Spanish royalty but a part of that decision is due to sheer bloody-mindedness—if one is writing about the Portuguese one ought to give them the courtesy of using their names properly! As for pronouncing them, it's sufficient to remember that "j" sounds like the "j" in "just" and "ão" usually is very much like "ow".

But I digress, as our high school history teacher used to say when I was growing up in San Diego with the children of people who had come halfway round the world to fish.

11

CHAPTER ONE

Santa Maria

IN THE AFTERNOON, the sun beats down on the old road that climbs up the hillside from the sea to the small town of Vila do Porto on the island of Santa Maria in the Azores. There is a newer road where the trucks and cars rush up a well-asphalted surface, and that is what you see as the ferry docks at the new harbor, which is protected from the Atlantic by a jetty formed of huge boulders. The old road, much narrower and more circuitous, is almost invisible because it is so overgrown. It is paved with small lava blocks and it's obvious that no motor vehicle has jounced up it in a long time. A wide stone parapet guards the down side, a silent suggestion of danger lurking on the curves during storms.

Walking up the road on a fine day, the odors of the brush covering the hillside rise around you with the warming air. About halfway up a cluster of fig trees, escapees from the garden of a nearby house now fallen to ruins, covers the side of the hill. The broad leaves make the trees a haven for birds which may be no more native to this island in the middle of the Atlantic than the fig. If you pause in the shade and look out over the ocean, you will see the seemingly limitless water that isolated this island and its eight sisters from humans until the early 1400s.

The road tells part of the story of how the Azores got here: the stone paving was cut from the hardened lava which bubbled up from the mid-Atlantic ridge perhaps eight million years old—a mere yesterday in geologic time. Santa Maria is the oldest of the archipelago and there has been no volcanic action here since people began visiting it. The story is different on São Miguel, where the ferry leaves from: not only are there volcanic craters filled with lakes, but local folk picnicking on one of them can cook their suppers in a few hours by burying stewpots in sand heated by steam from deep within the earth. And on Faial—

one of the trio of Azores 500 kilometers to the northwest—the earth's cholers exploded with force in 1957, sending thousands into exile. The Portuguese coast is nearly 1,000 kilometers to the east of Santa Maria. While mariners may have sighted the islands before the first official expedition to the Azores in 1427—islands in the mid-Atlantic show up on maps decades before—they, like the Madeiras and the Cape Verde islands, had never been inhabited. Yet within twenty years of the Portuguese landing on Santa Maria, a colony was established, and by the time Columbus returned from his world-changing voyage in 1493, he could stop at a town on the north of the island to fulfill a vow made during a storm at sea.

When the foundations of Vila do Porto were laid, Joan of Arc had recently led French armies against the English, the Swedish parliament was meeting for the first time, and the Moors still held much of Spain. Evidence of the town's age comes from its very location at the top of the hill. Most port cities, after all, have their roots on their waterfronts. Cities that relied on water traffic for a major part of their early economic activity might spread onto high ground as they grew, but usually they looked toward the sea or a river which led to it.

Yet here the emphasis appears to have been on building on the heights. Without a doubt there would have been installations at the anchorage at the bottom of the hill, but what exists on the waterfront now was built after Portugal joined the European Union in 1986. As you follow the old road to the top of the hill, though, you come across ruins of a church and buildings which date from the early eighteenth century, with timbers of a size that bear witness to forests of tall trees long since cut down. A plaque dates the ruins of the church and the fortress to 1732, some 300 years into the history of Vila do Porto. Nevertheless, until the advent of cars and trucks in the twentieth century, everything shipped in or out was transported up the hill by cart or by a strong human back—whole centuries of sweaty climbs and straining muscles.

Why not settle near the water? Professor José Curto of York University laughs when asked the question. For protection, of course. At the time Vilo do Porto was established, the Portuguese had been building a castle on every hill for centuries, he says, as they pushed the Moors out of their country and then defended it. In Lisbon today one sees the pattern. The Castelo São Jorge sits on top of one of the city's seven hills.

The height had been fortified since Roman times, and during Moorish rule, the fortress and its surroundings became a walled Muslim city. Defense is much easier when you can shoot arrows or cannon down on men struggling to climb a steep hillside.

The Moors were expelled from Portugal in 1255, nearly 250 years before they finally surrendered to the Spanish. Portugal's boundaries have changed very little in the more than 750 years since then. The last great battle over Portuguese territory was decided when a Spanish incursion was repulsed in 1380. You might think, therefore, that an isolated Portuguese outpost in the middle of the Atlantic without a wealth of spices, slaves or gold would be relatively safe from invasion, But for reasons related to the rather humdrum question of where to get wheat for bread, Santa Maria was a prize.

By the fourteenth century Portuguese fields weren't producing enough grain for the country's population. Historians blame bad agricultural management as well as withdrawal of land from cultivation by large landowners more interested in the courtly life than farming. Supplies had to be brought from farther afield, which was nothing new, in European history. For several hundred years Roman imported grain from Sicily, Egypt and elsewhere in Northern Africa. After the Roman Empire collapsed, the grain trade continued elsewhere with wheat from the Ukraine ending up in Constantinople, and wheat from Normandy being shipped to ports on the North Sea like Bruges. The preferred method to transport the grain was by water: the wind is free, which meant low transportation cost.

And when the Portuguese planted wheat on the Azores and on Madeira they found a bonanza. The fields were far more fertile than the exhausted ones at home. Not only had the soil never been tilled before, but its relatively recent volcanic origin meant that it was full of elements that encouraged good crops.

The first settlement on Santa Maria was near the water on the north side of the island, but within a few years Vila da Porto's location on the heights above the anchorage proved a wise choice. By stoning them from the heights, townspeople in 1480 successfully repelled an attack by Barbary pirates looking for wheat and other riches. There followed attacks by French and English corsairs during the next century and by Moors after that. The defence was not always successful; a group of

Some of the buildings on Santa Maria, like the Hermitage, date from the eighteenth century, and have been restored.

settlers were carried off in one of the Moorish attacks and sold into slavery.

This fear of outsiders was probably behind the rough welcome that Christopher Columbus received when he tried to anchor off Santa Maria on his way back from his first voyage in the stormy February of 1493. In his log he writes about the terrible tempest that battered his ships the *Niña* and the *Pinta*. (The third ship in his flotilla, the *Santa Maria*, had gone down off the coast of Hispaniola before they started the homeward voyage.) So rough were the seas that Columbus, who was a man of his time in the depth of his religious belief, vowed that were the ship saved, a pilgrimage would be made to Santa Maria de Guadalupe in Spain. To choose who would do it, he had a cupful of peas brought and one marked with a knife in the form of a cross. He went first to draw, and promptly picked the pea from the well-shaken peas. But the storm did not calm, and so he proposed another pilgrimage, this one to "Santa Maria di Loreto, which is in the province of Ancona, the land of the Pope, which is the house where Our Lady has performed and performs many great miracles." A sailor picked the marked pea that time, but since the storm continued to rage, the two promised pilgrimages appeared not to be enough. Columbus then proposed a third pilgrimage, to vigil at Santa Clara de Moguer one night and have a mass said: once again he picked the marked pea. Finally he made the whole crew "vow that the first land they reached they would all go in their shirts in procession to pray in a church under the invocation of Our Lady."

In his log book, Columbus muses about his great fear that he would not return with the news of his discoveries even though he was sure that because he had set out with God's favor he "ought not to fear the... tempest but ... weakness and anxiety would not allow (my) mind to become reassured," He was so worried that he and his ships might not survive that he wrote an account of his discoveries, wrapped it in waxed cloth and sealed it in a barrel. Then he had it thrown into the sea without telling his crew just what he had done, counting on their thinking that his actions were all part of his devotions.

The next day, the storm abated and over the next few days he and his sailors found themselves near Santa Maria. Making landfall was not an easy task, as fog and rain continued and the winds remained high, but finally they were able to anchor off the northern shore. When he sent a boat ashore, the inhabitants told his mariners they had never seen such a storm as the one which had raged for two weeks. So thankful was Columbus at reaching safety and at the friendly greeting, that he sent word that he and his crew would like to fulfill their pilgrimage vow then and there. Could the local priest say a mass of thanksgiving "at a small house which was near the sea, like a hermitage?" He would send half his crew and when they returned, he and the other half of the crew would go. While the first group was praying, the villagers, led by the captain of the settlement, Juan de Castaneda, descended on them and took them captive. It required considerable negotiation, including threats that King of Portugal, whom Columbus claimed as a friend, would not be pleased at their actions, before the settlers released his men.

The stormy weather continued, however; paradoxically, he later wrote, this encouraged Columbus. The contrast with the benevolent climate he'd found in the Indies, convinced him that he had found Paradise, the land of the East he'd been seeking. "The sacred theologians and learned philosophers well said that the earthly Paradise is at the end of the Orient, because it is a most temperate place," he wrote.

He wanted to get back to Spain with his news. Once his men were restored to him, he wasted no time in putting out to sea. He stopped in Lisbon, but not for long. That he was not sailing for the Portuguese has turned out to be a bit of an embarrassment for Portugal over the centuries. The weather had turned bad again, and putting into the Tagus estuary probably looked inviting, but there may have been an element of "Told you so" in his stop. Columbus had approached the Portuguese king twice in search of what would now be called venture capital before he turned to the Spanish monarchs for support. The Spanish were trying to catch up in the game of territorial expansion, now that the kingdoms of Aragon and Castile were finally united, and the Moors expelled. Portuguese explorers had been sailing down the coast of Africa for decades with the aim of reaching the Indies that way and it seems that the Portuguese king saw no reason to send out a feeler in another direction when he already had men and ships making headway in the search for the riches of the Indies.

But let's return to Santa Maria now, more than 500 years later. At the top of the hill, the old road up to Vila do Porto meets the new one. It's

Approach to Vila do Porto on Santa Maria in the Azores. Note the location of the old town on the heights above the anchorage.

not particularly wide—the population of the island is only 15,000 today so no superhighway is needed—but the center of the little town is filled with bustling twenty-first century life. Old buildings with the roofs fallen in still stand sentinel atop the steep hill on the ocean side, but toward the center of town the buildings have either been well maintained or restored. Satellite dishes dot roofs, farmers carry milk jugs and equipment on three-wheeled carts, and in the cantina you'll be addressed in English that might make you think you were in Toronto or Boston. That's because the owner spent twenty-four years in North America.

At the edge of the town, fields roll off toward even higher hills which rise in the center of the island. The landscape in summer is golden brown; the other side of the island is greener, because prevailing winds bring clouds which rise against the hills until their moisture condenses and falls as rain. Here on the rain-shadow side you might think you were in California, were it not for the odd ruined building which is older than anything there: the first California missions weren't begun until more than 400 years after Santa Maria was first settled, and 30 years after Santa Maria's now-ruined hermitage was built.

Santa Maria isn't only old buildings, fields and memories of a deep past, however. It is also home to an air traffic control center which monitors vast areas of the Atlantic Ocean from a facility which was built in the last two years of World War II. But even here the past plays an enormous role, because the facility owes its existence to a treaty signed in 1386 and consummated with marriage of the parents of the man responsible for sending out the ships that discovered the Azores. Infante Henrique, Prince Henry the Navigator, was the third son of Dom João I of Portugal and the English princess Philippa, the daughter of the influential English duke John of Gaunt.

Portugal was officially neutral during the Second World War. Long ruled by the ultra-conservative regime of dictator António de Oliveira Salazar, the country maintained cordial relations with fascist regimes in Spain, Italy and Germany during the 1930s. Once World War II broke out, Salazar refused to come out openly in favor of those regimes. For a long period, a good way to escape Europe was to leave from Lisbon by ship or air. At the end of *Casablanca*, you'll remember, Humphrey Bogart puts Ingrid Bergman on the plane for Lisbon with her husband, having handed over the precious exit permits he had in his possession. The message is clear; they would escape to the New World and resistance work, while Bogey and Claude Rains might or might not be able to join the Free French in Brazzaville in West Africa.

The film was released in 1943, just when secret negotiations were underway between the Portuguese and the British to allow the use of the Azores as way-stations for flights across the Atlantic. The air field on the island of Terceira was expanded, and a larger one constructed on Santa Maria, because 560 years earlier John of Gaunt and the Portuguese king "cordially agreed that if, in time to come, one of the kings or his heir shall need the support of the other, or his help, and in order to get such assistance applies to his ally in lawful manner, the ally shall be bound to give aid and succor to the other, so far as he is able (without any deceit, fraud, or pretence) to the extent required by the danger to his ally's realms, lands, domains, and subjects; and he shall be firmly bound by these present alliances to do this."

No matter that Portugal's last king had been removed from office in 1910, Salazar could see which way the wind was blowing in the conflict between the Allies and the Axis and chose secretly to bend the rules of neutrality. After discussions with Winston Churchill through intermediaries, Salazar gave the go-ahead to the presence of British military at the Terceira airport. But it seemed that all parties realized this was the mere thin edge of the wedge. The Santa Maria installation was designed to be a major staging area for moving men and equipment across the Atlantic to Europe. It involved large investment and presence on the part of the United States which, of course, in no way had been party to the treaty of 1386. The airfield was finished within days of the end of the war in Europe, so its major military use was in the demobilization of North American troops from the European front. The U.S. presence ended shortly after the war (it continues on Terceira in a modified form), but the base is still important as one of the two points of air traffic control over the southern part of the North Atlantic.

Of course, when Philippa married João I, no one would have guessed where the treaty signed just months before the wedding might lead. At issue then was the simple need to make a diplomatic alliance, and also to marry her off. By the standards of the time, at twenty-six she was rather old for a bride. Her hand had been offered to at least two other princes by her father, but in each case the noble had looked politely away. Apparently she had the reputation of being bookish and rather too pious. The British poet Geoffrey Chaucer, a friend of the family, had been her tutor. On the Portuguese throne she proved to be a rigorously virtuous woman.

There is one portrait which shows her as a pretty, pale young woman wearing an elaborate crown; her gaze is directed prayerfully toward heaven. Her light brown hair peeks out from under a white scarf that extends down her back. Her shoulders are covered with a red cape embroidered with gold designs, and lined with the sky blue that has become associated with the Virgin. She wears no jewelry, except for a round gold brooch which fastens her cape. She looks beautiful, as holy as an illustration in some Lives of the Saints. The painting, to judge from its style, was executed long after her death, but there is an authenticated painting of her wedding, dating from her time. No hair escapes her high headdress, and she poses with her new husband stiffly and unrealistically in the style of the fourteenth century. The scarlet-trimmed train of her white dress is held up by a young woman with a similar conical hat. Philippa is wearing a bejeweled necklace as she holds out her hand to be joined by the priest with that of João. He is resplendent in a lustrous black robe trimmed with fur or velvet. He wears a crown small enough to show his brown hair which contrasts with his red beard, and he is not the only red-bearded one. The bishop has a red beard too, as do the men immediately to his right and behind him. Obviously in the fourteenth century the genes of the north were prevalent in Portugal.

Philippa's renown has lasted for centuries. She is the only woman that the Salazar government saw fit to include in a grand monument to Portuguese explorers erected in 1940 for a World's Fair just outside Lisbon. It is called the *Padrão dos Descobrimentos,* after the carved stones, *padrões,* which the Portuguese always carried with them to leave as markers where they landed on their voyages of exploration. This group portrait brings together thirty-two of the most illustrious Portuguese explorers and Philippa, who, some say, was behind it all.

It is likely that Salazar and his friends included her because of her piety. When the monument was installed, Philippa's accomplishments—the children she bore and nurtured, the piety which led her to champion Portugal's wars against the Moors and to insist on high moral standards in the previously profligate Portuguese court—made her an appropriate inclusion in the eyes of the Salazar regime.

João I certainly did not have many sexual scruples as a young man. By the time they married, he had already had three illegitimate children by his mistress, despite the fact he'd taken a vow of chastity as the head of a religious order of crusading knights. Once married, though, (in fact, Philippa's father had to get special permission from the Pope for João to be relieved of his vow before the marriage could go ahead) he appears not to have strayed far during their nearly thirty years together. Philippa gave birth to their first child within a year (a girl who died in infancy) and over the next fifteen years bore eight more children, the last when she was forty-two. And what children! Her six sons are called the Illustrious Generation by the Portuguese, while the one girl who survived, Isabella, became a strong and influential woman in France.

The domestic climate that Philippa and João were reared in was characterized by political intrigue, arranged marriages and unbridled passion outside of wedlock. Philippa's mother died when she was about eight, and her father married a Castilian princess who gave him a claim to the throne of Castile. He had one daughter with her, but continued an affair he had been conducting with Katherine Swynford. A sister of Chaucer's wife, Katherine had been one of John of Gaunt's first wife's ladies-in-waiting and a governess, it seems, to young Philippa. Katherine eventually became John of Gaunt's third wife, and their four children were legitimized as adults.

Events were just as tempestuous in Portugal. João I himself was the only child of his father's liaison with a young woman, a romance that came after the older man's tragic love affair with Inês de Castro, one of his wife's ladies-in-waiting. João's father had three children with his first wife, two of whom lived to adulthood, but he much preferred Inês, who bore him four children. He was maneuvered into having Inês killed under circumstances that inspired several operas and a couple of plays. He looked for solace in the arms of someone else, with João I as the result.

Given the number of possible successors to the Portuguese throne, it's probably not surprising that after the death of João I's father, near civil war developed. The period 1383-85 is still called The Crisis today. When João I was crowned, Philippa's father decided to push his claim to the crown of Castile in part by getting Portugal involved. Philippa's wedding was, in fact, part of those negotiations, which included that agreement where England and Portugal agreed to come to each other's aid forever. When the king of Castile learned of the English pretender's plans, he invaded Portugal with a force of French archers.

In a battle whose description sounds a lot like the one at Agincourt 30 years later where Henry V with his "band of brothers" beat the French, the Portuguese, supported by English archers, overcame a Spanish force of 30,000 and 10,000 French cavalry. The French knights were heavily armed, and when their horses were shot out from under them by crack archers, they were finished off quickly on the battlefield. The battle of Aljubarrota ended the ambitions of Castile and other Spanish states to acquire Portugal. Now the Portuguese could look southward and west into the Atlantic. Philippa's sons would launch the Portuguese empire. That enterprise would be holy, she said as she lay dying of plague in 1415, just days before the first expedition set out to capture the North African town of Ceuta. She gave her sons swords and prayed with them. She predicted their victory in an endeavor that, some sources say, originated with her desire to bring what she considered the true faith to the world. She lies next to João I in the chapel at Batalha. Their effigies are side by side on the same raised tombstone, his right hand reaching over to hold her right hand in a touching sign of affection.

Some summer days the ferry from the larger, more populous island of São Miguel arrives in Santa Maria in the late morning and leaves in the afternoon. The travelers are in large part tourists, going to look around, perhaps stay the night, do some fishing, hike through the hills, and enjoy the solitude of a lovely, sparsely populated island. Despite being in middle of the Atlantic, it is legally a part of Europe since the Azores are a department of Portugal. Prices are quoted in euros, and you can get traffic reports from Lisbon and Porto on the local stations which transmit programming from the mainland on Radio e Televisão de Portugal (RTP).

Other passengers are people with family in the Azores. They or their parents left during one of the waves of immigration that pushed people from these islands to another part of the Portuguese dominions in the early days or, more recently, to opportunity in Brazil, Canada, and the United States. Some will be meeting relatives they haven't seen for a long time.

For those who are here for a short stay and must return on the afternoon ferry, the walk down the hill to the waterfront will be hot as the sun begins its glide down toward the ocean. People pause near the ruins of the old hermitage and look out at the sea. It seems to go on forever, this highway to fortune and adventure. But the ocean is, in most respects, profoundly indifferent to whomever rides its waves. It was there long before the European age of exploration, and it will continue into a future where the memories and lessons from Lusitania are forgotten.

CHAPTER TWO

Seafaring

ON A JULY DAY in the early twenty-first century, it is hard to believe just how dangerous the sea can be. The stretch of shore from which the most celebrated Portuguese voyages of exploration began is bright with sunlight glinting off the mingling waters of the River Tagus and the Atlantic Ocean. Tour buses stop at the Torre de Belém which has guarded the seaward approach to Lisbon for nearly 500 years, and at the nearby *Padrão dos Descobrimentos,* commemorating the Portuguese adventure. Visitors from around the world consult guide books, read historical markers and listen to explanations from tour guides about the glories of Portugal. This lovely water front park seems in stark contrast to the name this stretch along the river front has carried for centuries: the Praia das Lágrimas, the Beach of Tears, the Shore of Sorrows.

But the old name is apt and heavy with symbolism. One of the most quoted verses of the twentieth century poet Fernando Pessoa begins with the rhetorical question "Oh briny sea, how much of your salt comes from the tears of Portugal?" (*Ó Mar salgado, quanto do teu sal/ são lágrimas de Portugal !*) And a *fadista* sings of the women in black who mourn the men who will never return, their tears making the ocean's water salty.

This is the point from which Vasco da Gama and his crew left for a world-changing voyage to India on July 8, 1498. Chances are it was as nice a day as this one: the epic poem that describes da Gama's voyage speaks of "gentle breezes" and July is noted for being a hot and sunny month on this stretch of the Portuguese coast. Yet da Gama's departure was a defining moment the Portugal's history, which carries much sadness along with the glory. A small country with never more than a population of 2.2 million during the period of its greatest world

View from the Torre de Belém, the tower which guarded the entrance to the anchorage at Lisbon, just off the Praia das Lágrimas, from which Vasco da Gama left for his world-changing voyage to India in 1498.

expansion, Portugal sent out a staggering number of men to fish, to explore, to colonize. Indeed, between 1500 and 1750, the total ran to about 1.5 million, or an average of 6,000 a year, year in, year out. It was as if the country annually lost the population of a good-sized regional town or the equivalent of a small army. How many came back is not clear. Mortality on the long voyages—to go to India and back often took three years in the days of sailing ships—was frequently fifty percent or higher, and once arrived, disease and the attraction of local women claimed many more.

Walking along the shore at Belém today it is possible to imagine what those sailors were leaving behind. Across the river rise low hills that are now covered with fields separated by rows of trees. The fishing village of Caparica lies nearly directly opposite, and on the highest point a stature of Jesus Christ, Cristo Rei, looks down on the river. Back then the fields were proably covered with the *matagal*, the Portuguese version of the low scrub forest found around the world on coasts where summers are hot and dry and winters, mild and wet. If the wind were right on the July day, Vasco da Gama set sail, a hint of the fragrance rising from the aromatic shrubs might have been smelled by sailors on the river as the ships weighed anchor and went out on the tide.

The Tagus is one of the great rivers of Europe, and its has been home to humans for millennia. Not only have fossils of our nearest relations the Neanderthals been found not far from Lisbon, but there is also abundant evidence humans found refuge in Portugal when the great sheets of ice covered much of Europe during the last Ice Age.

The river itself runs through Spain for more than half of its 1,038-kilometer (645-mile) course, providing water for Toledo, Salamanca and Madrid. It cuts gorges through mountains, fills valleys, and waters towns and fields as it makes its way west and south and west again. Finally it spreads out, some seventy-five kilometers (47 miles) from the sea as if waiting before sending its water through the narrows to be lost in the Atlantic. Like the rivers of the Great Valley of California which fill San Francisco Bay, the tides rise and fall in the Tagus estuary, providing food and refuge for a rich wonder of birds and shore and marine creatures. Lisbon sits about 30 kilometers (18 miles) from the open sea, partially protected from the storms that sweep in off the ocean by the hills which form the northern shore of the river. The land to the south is lower except for the hills facing the ocean and which now anchor the 25th of April suspension bridge that soars across the river.

Today the main docks of the great port are east of the Praia das Lágrimas. The docks are equipped with the cranes and machines needed to load and unload cargo from huge freighters. Ferries run back and forth, cruise ships dock regularly, and pleasure craft sail gaily on the blue water. These are, of course, modern manifestations of human skill in using water as a way of getting around, a skill which bears looking at closely by anyone interested in the Portuguese. After all, their adventure would never have happened had they not gone down to the sea in ships.

Some 40,000 years ago humans began traveling the oceans. The islands of Southeast Asia and Australia were settled that long ago, and must have involved travel by some sort of man-made vessel, probably dugout canoes and rafts. Sails show up on Egyptian pottery created 4,000 years ago while the grave of Egyptian Queen Hatshepsut memorializes a sailing expedition down the east coast of Africa in 1500 BCE. Rock carvings in China nearly that old also show boats with sails.

At first sails were just an auxiliary source of power, with most of the work being done by current in the case of rivers, or oarsmen, or

The Egyptians used sales for some of their voyages. This drawing dates from 1500 BC and depicts Queen Hatshepsut's expedition to the east coast of Africa.

men and animals on shore who pulled the boat from a tow path. But when early mariners hoisted a sail and then tried to keep it straight, they discovered that when the sail was held at an angle to the wind, the boat would be propelled diagonally forward. In Northern Europe and in China the preferred sail shape was square, but sailors around the Red Sea discovered that rigging the boat with a triangular sail or sails that could be easily swiveled on the mast made a slip-sliding forward course—called tacking—easier to undertake. The small, quick, triangular-sailed Egyptian felucca and dhow of the Arabs were perfect for navigating along the coast where a zigzag course into the wind was frequently necessary. On larger ships, the triangular shape was later adapted to become the lateen sail which improved maneuverability of ships, setting the stage for the Portuguese voyages of exploration.

In this day when even cell phones come equipped with GPS and cars tell you what highway exit to take, the difficulties encountered by past travelers are hard to imagine. Even setting off in a small boat along a coast you knew could be tricky: only a few decades ago the Coast Guard had to rescue my fifteen-year-old sister and a friend when a sudden gale on San Diego Bay blew the one-sailed boat they were in off course. In the truly olden times, traveling farther to some place new must have required considerable courage—or bad luck. A storm, a simple shift in the wind, coastwise currents that change with the season—any of these might mean being swept long distances. The Greeks, Romans and Phoenicians did cross the Mediterranean—it's 1200 kilometers from Rome to Alexandria, where the Romans picked up pepper brought from India—but the distance when the captain navigated out of sight of land was not great. But with a chart, or the living memory found in a good pilot's head, plus some basic astronomical knowledge, captains were surprisingly successful even without magnetic compasses, let alone devices for figuring out precisely where they were.

Indeed magnetic compasses arrived in Europe only in the eleventh century. That was also about the time Muslim traders perfected a device to judge latitude by taking a fix on the pole star and determining how high above the horizon it was. The idea of circling the earth with a grid of latitude and longitude lines was not new, however. That the world was round was a concept accepted by all serious Greek thinkers, with Aristotle and others calculating the earth's circumference to within five to ten percent of what it is actually. Later Claudius Ptolemy, assuming the world was a sphere, was able to map the known part using grids based on degrees, an idea inspired by the Babylonians who had long before divided circles into 360 degrees. This scheme for measuring could be easily transposed to the vault of the heavens where the progression of the stars across the grid becomes obvious. In the course of one night alone, stars rise in the east and traverse the sky as the sun does during the day, and groups of stars appear and disappear from night to night as the seasons pass.

Star maps have been particularly useful to voyagers for the last millennium or so because stars in the Northern Hemisphere now seem to move around a fixed point in the sky, the North, Polaris or Pole Star. That's a happy cosmic accident, since the axis of the earth's rotation wobbles a bit over a 25,700 year cycle and in the times of the ancients Polaris was not as reliable a guide as it is today. Homer has Calypso tell Odysseus to keep the constellations with the North Star to his left side when he wants to leave her island, but the North Star would not have truly indicated north then. Having it as an infallible guide gave Portuguese navigators a measure of confidence in the Northern Hemisphere they did not have when they began to venture into the seas of the Southern Hemisphere. It is possible there to determine which direction is south from the objects in the sky, but there is no guide as user-friendly as the North Star.

The North Star also allows you to figure out just how far north on the earth's surface you are, since the height of the North Star in the sky equals roughly your latitude. That is, if Polaris appears to be about 40 degrees above the horizon, you're about 40 degrees north latitude. That knowledge would be quite useful if you were headed for Rome (41°54'N), Barcelona (41°23'N), Istanbul (known to the Ancients as Byzantium, 41°02'N), or Lisbon (39°30'N.) Even the Azores lie near this band of latitude, stretching from 36°55' to 39°45'N.

Until the eighteenth century, however, there was no reliable way to determine how far east or west you were. It took the invention of a portable, reliable timepiece to do the calculations necessary, noting the time and comparing star positions with those from known longitudes. Columbus twice tried to do so during his voyages to the New World when a lunar eclipse provided moments when determining longitude was theoretically possible, but both times he failed miserably.

The navigators of old had a few other tools. One was a weighted line to throw over the side to measure depth of the water, very important when sailing close to shore or where reefs and undersea rocks were known to exist. The weight was hollowed out and filled with tallow so it would pick up sediments from the bottom. From the sand and gravel bits that stuck, an experienced sailor could frequently guess how far offshore the ship was when fog reduced visibility. Sounds heard in the fog itself helped too: the distant crash of breakers against rocks or the softer, more sibilant sound of waves on a sandy shore told a great deal. Farther out to sea, birds carried clues about location with them as they flew overhead. The Azores got their name from the sightings of early mariners who noted raptors (*açores* in Portuguese or goshawks) circling in skies far beyond the range of hawks which lived on the continent. Islands had to be nearby, the sailors knew, so the lookout was alerted to be particularly vigilant as he scanned the horizon.

Another tool was a technique to figure out how fast the ship was traveling. When ships sailed in sight of land, the passing coastline was all that was needed to get a good idea of speed, supplemented by skill developed over time in watching how fast bits of seaweed, feathers and other flotsam floated past. But for situations when the shore is not visible and floating objects are not present, another method was developed, one which has echoes today. A wooden panel attached to a rope knotted at fixed intervals (the standard was 47 feet 3 inches or 14.4018 meters) was thrown into the water from the stern of the vessel. One sailor counted the knots as they played out through his fingers and another timed the process with a 30-second sandglass. The unit of distance was therefore called a knot, with one knot working out 20.25 inches per second, or 1.85166 kilometers per hour, which is almost exactly the distance of a minute of latitude.

With this estimate of how fast a ship was sailing and a compass it was possible to chart a ship's course by the method called dead reckoning (often shortened to DR and used extensively, buttressed with better tools for measuring speed and location, until there was widespread availability of GPS at the beginning of the twenty-first century.) The calculation began at a known spot on a map: Columbus, for example, began his chart for his first voyage at the Canary Islands. If the wind blew steadily from the right direction, charting the course was easy, amounting to little more than measuring out the distance traveled along a straight line (called a rhomb line) beginning at the departure point. But if the wind blew at cross purposes and the ship had to tack back and forth to keep moving, the course was more complicated. Each change in direction had to be taken into account as well as the speed of the ship and the time traveled in that direction. The result would be a zigzag course on the chart, tending—if the calculations were right—in the general direction the captain wanted the ship to go. He might be able to check his calculations against the North Star, although taking a reading when the sea was rough and the sky cloudy was often impossible. Many was the captain who found himself far from where he thought he was when he finally saw land, even on the Mediterranean.

At the Straits of Gibraltar the Pillars of Hercules guard the western end of that sea. Beyond them, many ancient texts said, was a dark, forbidding, dangerous sea without end. This is not to say that mariners did not venture through the straits and turn north along the coast. The Phoenicians, based in North Africa, sailed as far as Cornwall in order to obtain tin, a metal necessary for making the alloy which gave its name to the Bronze Age. Documents also suggest that as early as the fourth century BCE one intrepid adventurer, Phateus, sailed as far as the Scandinavian peninsula and returned to Greece. By Roman times the idea that St. James might be able to sail around the Iberian peninsula in a small boat to Campostella on the northern coast of Spain was not so foreign as to seem impossible—only miraculous.

By then, several towns in what is now Portugal had been in existence for hundreds of years. The two great port cities of Porto and Lisbon date at least from the time Rome wrested the territory from Phoenician control in the third century BCE. Legend has it that Lisbon gets its name from that great traveler Ulysses; the settlement shows up on old Roman maps as Ulissipo and on Greek ones as Olissipo. (The Romans called the larger area which now corresponds more or less with Portugal, Lusitania. The name is of unknown origin but popular belief connects it with a Lusus, a companion of the Roman God of revelry, Bacchus.)

The geographer Strabo wrote that the Tagus estuary abounded in fish and oysters. The ruins of a Roman pottery across the river from Lisbon testify to a nearby population big enough to require thousands of pots. When municipal workers on a sewage project in the 1990s discovered the pottery dump, they uncovered a wealth of broken pots, indicating how large the community was. In addition to bigger ships which must have occasionally come from elsewhere in the Roman territories, a flotilla of small boats fished the calmer water of the estuary and occasionally put out to sea.

After the fall of Rome, the power vacuum was filled by the rise of small Germanic and Celtic fiefdoms. Muslim invaders arrived in the ninth century. While the thrust of the Muslim advance was across the Mediterranean and into the southern part of the Iberian peninsula, the ships of the conquering Moors also dared to go beyond Gibraltar and into the Dark Sea that their tradition, not unlike that of the Greeks, held lay beyond.

But what was there, in fact, in the uncharted waters of the Atlantic? A wealth of fish, rumors of islands, and hints of riches.

About the same time that Moors succeeded in controlling much of the Mediterranean, the Vikings began sailing through the Straits into the sea that the people who lived around its rim considered the middle of the world. Both Norse and Muslim mariners amassed great knowledge of the winds and currents, some of which had been learned from sailors of other maritime traditions. By the mid-fourteenth century maps and marine charts included islands in the Atlantic. The Azores show up on one such map, the Laurentian *portulan*, dating from 1351. Like other portulans, it notes not only the outlines of landforms, but also winds and currents.

"The place where these islands lie cannot be found by intention, but only by chance, because ships sail on the sea where the winds take them, and navigation is dependent upon knowing the direction the wind blows, and where it blows from," wrote the Arab chronicler Ibn Khaldun about the Canary Islands, the first of the Atlantic islands to be "discovered" off the east coast of Africa. The fickleness of the wind is underlined by the fact the Canaries had been settled hundreds if not a thousand years before by light-skinned people who spoke a language containing many Berber words, that is, by people who probably came from North Africa. They had been isolated for so long, however, that their culture had lost the skill of using boats, even though on exceptionally clear days the peaks of the mountain on Tenerife can be seen from the African coast.

Yet, at the beginning of the fifteenth century figurative winds of change were blowing in Europe that would lead to harnessing the real winds so that mariners could sail where they wanted to go, seeking out lands obscured by legend. What was required was something completely counter-intuitive: to sail away from land in order to catch winds going in a different direction and ride them home.

Infante Henrique, called the Navigator, the third son of Queen Philippa and João I, did not live to see this conquest of the winds, but that they were conquered is directly due to his support. Born in 1394, he was third in line to the throne, after his brother Duarte (born in 1391, named after his great-grandfather Edward III of England) and Pedro, Duke of Coimbra (born in 1392, named after his grandfather Pedro I of Portugal). Henrique's intelligence and courage were recognized early. He was only twenty-one when he and his older brothers joined an expedition led by their father to Ceuta, a town just inside the Straits of Gibraltar on the African side. It had been in Muslim hands for more than 500 years, and João I, encouraged by the pious Philippa, considered its capture to be part of a grand design to push back the power which was collectively called the Moors. By this time Portugal had existed as a nation free from Moorish control for more than 100 years, although a large part of the rest of the Iberian peninsula was still in Muslim hands, and the kingdoms of Castile and Aragon would not be united for another generation.

João I's motivation for this expedition was in part religious. Like many other leaders in the Christendom of the times, he took seriously the idea of "freeing" lands held by Muslim powers. That Portugal was more or less at peace with Spain also meant that the country had men who were free to fight in military expeditions elsewhere. Many of them were the sons of men who had risen in station in life after the last conflict with Spain which saw many of the old nobility killed in battle. This younger group were keen to win their spurs and show their valor.

But there were economic reasons as well. The pattern of land ownership that continues in modern Portugal today was by then already well-established. The northern part of the country is relatively well watered. It is also hilly, which encourages small farmsteads. The south, however, is much dryer and more suited to crops like wheat grown on larger holdings. Yet, as already noted, food production was falling because many of the nobles and religious orders who owned the farms were more interested in affairs of the court or the church than in farming. Therefore getting control of the wheat trade with access to the granaries of North Africa which had helped feed Europe since Roman times was a major goal. Ceuta was a trans-shipment point for wheat.

Just as important, the port was also one of the northern terminals of the caravan routes which brought gold, slaves and ivory from the other side of the Sahara. Some economic historians assert that the need for gold itself in the fourteenth and fifteenth centuries is sufficient to account for the quest for the shiny metal in Africa and elsewhere. The Portuguese did not need it in order to make essential things—jewelry and sculpture were its main use until recent times when gold became important in dentistry and electronics. When it comes to intrinsic value, iron is much more useful, but has never prompted the equivalent to the crazy gold rushes that have occurred many times over the ages. No, gold's importance lies in the fact that it—like silver—has come to be accepted as a universally accepted token of exchange. The two metals are relatively rare, are easily worked, don't rust or mold, are hard to counterfeit and can be divided into parts without much trouble. Other materials with the same properties have been just as important as tokens of value: indeed, in West Africa cowry shells were more important than gold until well after the arrival of the Portuguese, which worked to their advantage once they began to explore the coast.

But that's getting ahead of the story.

There were ideological motivations behind João I's North African invasion. too. Dismissing his desire to bring Christianity to what he would call the Infidel is as important a mistake as saying that the Israeli-Palestinian conflict today is really about water and land, and not about what many Jews believe was promised to them. The concept of Islamic jihad (from the Arabic word for "effort" on behalf of God and Islam) had given moral authority to Moorish warriors during the conflicts of the previous several centuries, as well as to Muslim traders who followed their conquests.

At the turn of the fourteenth century João I, Philippa and their sons sincerely believed, as did most of their contemporaries, in the literal truth of the Bible. Eden had existed, and might still. It was said to lie where four great rivers began, which might be in the heartland of Africa, a continent of people who either had been captured by the Infidel Moor or who still worshipped idols. The narrative that the Portuguese told themselves meant that their battle at Ceuta was an affair of honor and the true faith. For Henrique it augured well for his future. Indeed, it was completely in keeping with the predictions made at his birth by the court's official astrologer, that he would devote himself to "great and noble conquests and to the uncovering of secrets previously hidden from men." (If there was a contradiction between faith in God and expecting enlightenment through reading the stars, few among Henrique's contemporaries noticed. That Henrique's brother Duarte ascended to the throne at a particularly inauspicious moment, astrologically speaking, and died a short time after, reinforced the belief of those who thought that God's will might be understood through plotting the stars and planets.)

The battle of Ceuta was a victory for the Portuguese, but not before a series of mishaps at sea that might have convinced the superstitious that Portugal's future was not maritime. The galleys arrived before the supply ships, soldiers were dreadfully seasick, plague broke out, and sailors had problems maneuvering off the coast. Nevertheless, João I's force triumphed, in part because he and many of his captains were seasoned soldiers whose military experience went back to the successful campaigns against the Castilians. His sons were valiant, and he knighted them on the battlefield. That was a mythic moment that Henrique long remembered, and tried unsuccessfully to reprise in his middle age.

In the years following Ceuta, Henrique took the lead in encouraging Portuguese maritime ventures. Good Christian son of a devout mother that he was, his motivation was partly religious, but from the very beginning he realized that there were fortunes to be made in exploration. At various times in the centuries since his death, he has been lionized as a "veray parfit gentil knight," to use Chaucer's phrase. Historians in the nineteenth century painted him as a romantic figure, devoted to research into astronomy, geography and mathematics, dedicated to the discovery of new worlds as well as the conversion of the Infidel. However, like most royals, Henrique expected to live on income from his holdings, and when the opportunity came to increase them, he was not shy to take advantage of it.

After the glorious victory, his father appointed him the administrator for Ceuta. Rather than becoming a treasure house for riches from the other side of the Sahara and grain from North Africa, however, it became a drain on the kingdom. It had to be supplied by sea, since the surrounding territory was controlled by Muslims. The square-rigged merchant ships that usually were favored for cargo proved too cumbersome to move easily through the Straits of Gibraltar, so Henrique and his aides came to rely on the smaller lateen-rigged caravel, developed originally for offshore fishing, which was fast and easier to maneuver. Because each caravel could carry less than a larger square-rigged ship, however, the fleet had to be enlarged, with dozens more ships. That meant that when Henrique began to think of longer voyages in the Atlantic there were many ships ready to become the workhorses of exploration. By the time he was in his mid-thirties, Henrique personally owned several caravels and controlled more. He gave his captains permission to attack Muslim vessels—the infidel enemy anywhere was seen as fair game—or even ships owned by Christians who were thought to be trading with the enemy.

Among his captains was Gonçalo Velho, a friar of the Order of Christ, which were the Portuguese successors to the crusading order of Knights Templar. When Henrique decided to send ships looking for islands rumored to be in the Atlantic, Velho became one of his stalwart captains, later leading the movement to settle the Azores.

The Madeira archipelago—520 kilometers (323 miles) west of Africa and 1,000 kilomters (621 miles) southwest of mainland Portugal—was the first of the "new" islands that Henrique claimed, however. The islands show up on more than one map from the middle of the fourteenth century, but two of Henrique's captains came across them again when they were blown off course in 1419. Henrique's biographer Peter Russell speculates that the reason the Madeiras were not visited earlier by Italian or Iberian traders who very likely knew of them was because they were known to be uninhabited and the traders were looking for slaves. The Canaries were far more interesting to them precisely because they were settled, and Henrique also attempted to claim them.

The first group of settlers arrived on Madeira in the 1420s, intending to clear the land and grow wheat on the heavily forested island which takes its name for the Portuguese word for wood. In a pattern that was to be repeated again and again as Europeans advanced into the New World, clearing the land had tragic effects ecologically. One chronicle of the period says that fires set intentionally escaped control and burned for a long time (one source says seven years), making a beacon that could be seen far out to sea. Another reports that in the first years of cultivation, the fields produced wheat in a ratio of seventy to one, that is seventy grains harvested to one sowed, but that within fifty years the ratio dropped to thirty or forty to one. The settlers included members of the lower nobility, among them the parents of Christopher Columbus's wife. They contributed to the ecological damage: Columbus's son wrote that his grandfather introduced one female rabbit with her brood to the nearby island of Porto Santo. The rabbits were so prolific that the island was completely denuded of green within a year and colonization had to wait until the rabbit population crashed and vegetation returned.

Nevertheless the archipelago began producing wheat, grapes and vast quantities of timber; one source says that in Portugal itself buildings taller than a couple of stories became possible for the first time because previously not enough lumber had been available to build them. Logging also provided timbers to build the many ships needed for expanding Portuguese trade and exploration. In a relatively short time, however, that source was exhausted and the Portuguese had to look farther afield, particularly for tall, straight trunks big enough in circumference to serve as masts. The Russian term for the meter-thick logs of old growth forest is *karabel'nie sosni*, or caravel pines, suggesting just how wide-ranging that search became.

After timber, sugar became a major export. Sugar cane was introduced during the first decade of settlement and by the time Henrique died in 1460, Madeira had become a major supplier to Europe, with Henrique as master of the island, profiting from the revenues. When the Azores began to be settled in the early 1430s, Santa Maria and São Miguel, where the first settlers arrived, did not seem as inviting as Madeira, but became great producers of wheat.

But neither of these groups of islands was a source of riches like gold, spices or silk, nor had they pagan or Muslim natives whom Henrique and his friends might be able win over for Christ. To pursue those twin goals, they would have to look farther, to explore the West coast of Africa, and to seek, while they were about it, those rivers which were supposed to flow from Eden.

But, as ancient tradition had cautioned about the dangers beyond the Pillars of Hercules, maritime lore in Henrique's time warned that south of the Canaries the sea was impassable beyond Cabo Bojador on the northwest coast of Africa. Reefs, rocks, and rushing currents were supposed to scuttle any ship which dared to round the promontory located about 220 kilometers (120 nautical miles) due south of a headland on one of the Canary Islands. "Most mariners had heard it said that any Christian who passed Bojador would infallibly be changed into a black, and would carry to his end this mark of God's vengeance on his insolent prying," one of Henrique's biographers writes. The Arab tradition said a Green Sea of Night began there, while cartographers who had nothing else to go on filled the seas with monsters ready to grab whomever dared to venture farther down the coast.

In order to find treasure and to seek out more souls to save from the Infidel, Henrique sent out as many as fifteen expeditions to round the Cabo Bojador. All were unsuccessful until Gil Eanes, not a seasoned mariner, but one of Henrique's squires, succeeded on his second attempt in 1434, captaining a small fishing boat of the barca class down the coast. There he found a point extending forty kilometers (twenty-five miles) out to sea, with high surf and currents on the north side and shallows nearby, as well as prevailing winds that make it hard to turn back to the north. But he encountered no sea monsters or impossible and impassable seas, and the barrier to southward travel turned out to be more psychological than physical.

Over the next fifteen years a number of ships sailed farther and farther south along the west coast of Africa discovering, in addition, the Cape Verde islands far out to sea. By the time Henrique died, the Atlantic coastline had been rather reliably mapped down to eight degrees north of the equator.

It was not until after his death, however, that the Portuguese mariners made the startling, counter-intuitive discovery of how to use the prevailing winds in the South Atlantic in order to go south and eventually east around the tip of Africa. In what is considered the most important navigational advance of the era, they learned that by sailing westward away from Africa, they could go east by executing what came to be known as the *volta do mar*, the sea turn. After sailing south to the latitudes of the Canaries, they would allow the prevailing winds from the east to carry them far out into the Atlantic where after tacking south, they could pick up winds blowing from the west in the Southern Hemisphere. This sent them back to the east again, toward Africa and regions that where Europeans had never before sailed.

While Arab traders and others had sailed the waters off the east coast of Africa and knew them quite well, and West African warriors and fishermen travelled locally on the ocean on the west coast, there is no evidence that any mariner, foreign or African, had sailed the continent's west coast extensively. Yet within eight years after the discovery of the *volta da mer*, Portuguese mariners had conquered the sea lanes. In 1487-88 Barthelmeu Dias rounded the Cape of Good Hope by following the *volta da mer* winds, entered the Indian Ocean and then returned to Lisbon to tell the tale. The race to the Indies was won.

Among those who sailed with the Portuguese during the years of incursions farther and farther into the Atlantic was a sailor who would challenge that claim, Christopher Columbus. He shipped on at least one Portuguese voyage to the Gold Coast of Africa, probably in the 1470s, and, says his biographer Samuel Eliot Morison, he surely learned much "from his Portuguese shipmates, who were the world's finest mariners of that era." Because he knew from first-hand experience the great interest of the Portuguese in exploration, in 1484 he broached the idea of a voyage to the East by going west to the king, João II, Henrique's grand-nephew, who was then in the first years of his reign. Morison says Columbus had a shopping list of things he wanted from the king including three caravels and a title of nobility. João II, who even then was committed to trying to reach India by going around Africa, said no, although he gave his blessing in 1485 to a voyage west proposed by two mariners who didn't ask for help up front. They apparently set sail from Terceira in the Azores where the prevailing winds were against them, and it is there, Morison says, that they disappear from the record.

João II possibly had this unsuccessful voyage in mind when Columbus approached him a second time with his idea that it would be possible to reach Japan by sailing west. But the mariner's timing wasn't propitious. When he journeyed to Lisbon to discuss Portuguese royal support once again, he arrived just in time to witness Dias' triumphant return with the news that it was perfectly feasible to go around Africa to get to India. What is more, shortly afterwards news came from a Portuguese adventurer of his success in trekking overland across Egypt and then sailing in Arab vessels from the east coast of Africa to India. The Portuguese monarch, who now knew that there were two ways to get to the East, politely refused Columbus's request. Columbus turned to Ferdinand and Isabella who jointly governed their kingdoms of Castile and Aragon. They agreed to support Columbus, making him the Admiral of the Ocean Sea, and so the scene was set for the famous voyage of 1492.

North Americans are more likely to know about this discovery than the Portuguese ones, but was it really such an accomplishment? Daniel Boorstin writes in his fascinating book *The Discoverers* that in terms of difficulty, the Portuguese voyages were much more impressive. They were sailing far from the sight of land, and in latitudes where the very heavens were different from the ones that guided sailors around the Mediterranean and up the coast of Europe. Columbus, Boorstin points out, was sailing not into the unknown, but following a plan that came down from antiquity. Like the Ancient Greeks, he knew the earth was round, although he was mistaken on what its circumference was, and thought the Orient was a lot closer than it is. He also was aware of traditions holding that fishermen and other mythic figures had found land to the West: it's possible that he may have heard tales of Viking voyages as well as fishing expeditions to the Grand Banks off Newfoundland.

The Portuguese explorers, however, headed south toward countries which were considered unreachable, past barriers where all information indicated violent currents and where infernal headlands threatened. "The immediate effects of (the Portuguese explorers') voyages were incomparably more fulfilling than those of Columbus (who) promised the fabled cities of Japan and India, but ... reached only uncertain savage shores." Boorstin compares Columbus's trip with Vasco da Gama's voyage to India: Columbus went 2600 miles (4000 kilometers) to the westward "before a fair wind" in thirty-six days at sea, but Vasco da Gama's voyage lasted nearly a year and took him and his ships across the Southern Atlantic, doubling the Cape of Good Hope, up the eastern coast of Africa and then across the Indian Ocean to the West coast of India.

Over time a river's shore will shift, and this obviously has happened since the summer night when da Gama and his crew prayed in the Monastery of Jerónimos, the Mosteiro dos Jerónimos, before they set sail. Then the monastery was a modest sanctuary a few steps from the water's edge, but now it sits a 10 minute stroll from the river. The formal gardens of Praça do Imperio, planted in 1940 for a major international exposition, spread out in front. Flowers from places where the Portuguese explored, notably the blue Agapanthus, a native of southern Africa, and scarlet cannas from Brazil, provide splashes of color in the carefully mowed grass. Boxwood hedges and neatly trimmed trees surround a large fountain in the center whose jets of water send the sounds of coolness into the air on summer afternoons. On summer evenings colored lights dance on the water, adding another level to the enjoyment.

Da Gama wouldn't recognize the place. The modest monastery where they prayed has been transformed into the long and elaborately decorated Mosteiro complex containing church, cloister, library and museum. It, and the Torre were proclaimed a UNESCO World Heritage Site in 1983, They exemplify "Portuguese art at its best" and are reminders of "the great maritime discoveries that laid the foundation of the modern world," UNESCO said.

Vasco da Gama's last moments on the shores of the River Tagus were immortalized in the great Portuguese epic poem, *The Lusiads*. Written by Luis Vaz de Camões, a contemporary of Miguel Cervantes and William Shakespeare, the poem tells the story of the Portuguese and their conquest of the sea, their successful sortie to India, and their return to Lisbon under da Gama's captaincy. It is a work of art that defines the Portuguese intellectual and national character. That it was written in the sixteenth century does not make it any less relevant today.

Camões gave this stretch of riverfront its name, the Praia das Lágrimas. The tears that he described being shed as friends and family of da Gama's crew watched them prepare to leave were among first of torrents to flow. Only a third—or fewer, depending on what account you read—of Vasco da Gama's sailors survived to return to Portugal two years after they left. Nearly 500 years later Camões's words were used as a background to newsreels of young Portuguese soldiers embarking for the last colonial wars in Africa, bloody conflicts which debilitated the nation and which led to the nearly bloodless revolution at home in the 1970s. That juxtaposition of sometimes misguided heroism and ultimate good sense has marked the history of Portugal and the Portuguese wherever they traveled and settled around the world.

Step inside the chapel at the Mosteiro on this hot July afternoon and you will find the interior cool and shady. If you wait until a lull between the tour groups you may find it a place to rest and meditate on what this small nation set out to do, and what it has done. It is extraordinarily fitting that just inside the chapel are two tombs with life size effigies on top. One is that of Camões, the other, Vasco da Gama.

The workhorse of the Portuguese explorers, the caravel was small and maneuverable.

[CHAPTER THREE]

Spices and Souls

Vasco da Gama did not die in Lisbon, however. He died in 1524 on the west coast of India during his third voyage out, more than a quarter century after his first trip. By that time the Portuguese were the uncontested rulers of the seas from Africa to the Spice Islands, beyond what is now Indonesia, in the western Pacific. The church at Fort Kochi where Da Gama was first buried is far less elaborate than the monumental Mosteiro dos Jerónimos. It still stands, not far from the entrance to the harbor of Kochi (formerly called Cochin) on the Malabar Coast in Kerala state.

Even when a breeze is blowing off the Indian Ocean, just steps away, it is hot and humid here. To the south is a parade ground where centuries of military men have drilled. Right now however, the field is buzzing with young men playing, or watching, a cricket match. Nearby is a grave-yard where the moss-covered monuments inscribed in English and Dutch bear witness to the other colonial powers which held this rich coast after the Portuguese. Several stately houses are set back from the street. Built for officials of various governments, most have been turned into hotels or inns for the tourist trade. Along the sea front a row of kiosks provides food and drink for visitors on weekends and holidays. Families find the beach good for picnicking but the waves, no matter how hot the day, are not for swimming. The water is polluted, as is the water of Lake Vembanad, on the other side of the peninsula. The problems of the twenty-first century are very present, even in this part of India which has not only been a source of immense wealth over the centuries, but is now the healthiest and best educated region in the enormous country.

Fifteen hundred years ago the coastline was covered with man-groves, those big trees whose intertwining roots shelter fish and shrimp

43

and other wildlife. They trapped the silt washing down from the Western Ghat mountains. Indeed scientists say the whole of this low-lying countryside owes its existence to the trees since they kept the silt, sand and gravel from washing away under the constant barrage of waves rolling in from the Arabian Sea. Several large rivers drain the mountains, spreading out when they near sea level and forming what are called today the Backwaters, a region of interconnected lakes and lagoons which in the past were the major highway for transport of people and goods.

The harbors on the Malabar Coast have been busy since antiquity. One of the principle commodities is black pepper, native to the Western Ghats. Today salt and pepper are standard on the tables of most North American and European households, and the waiter in a restaurant who wants to grind black pepper on your salad or your main course can seem a bit pretentious, given how common the condiment is. In the past, however, pepper's piquant taste was so rare that only the affluent could afford it. Finding a new way of getting it to market in Europe was one of the major motivations behind Vasco da Gama's trips east.

Trade in pepper across the Indian Ocean by sail began at least as early as the first century CE, if not before. That was when Arab mariners— in a navigational development as important as the Atlantic *volta do mar* discovered by the Portuguese in the 1480s— found that they could ride the winds of the south-west monsoon from June to September from the Horn of Africa to India and then sail back on the northeast winds which prevail for most of the rest of the year. The ancient geographer Strabo says that a yearly expedition from the Roman Empire left with 100 or more ships from the northern end of the Gulf of Hormuz, and sailed across to Kerala to bring back the spice.

At what point the black pepper plant was domesticated is not clear, but botanists suspect that it goes back 2,500 years or more; wild pepper is still found in the mountains, but selective breeding has developed many varieties. Peppercorns are berries of a vine with oval leaves that looks rather like that easy-to-grow houseplant, the philodendron. The variety shown in the illustration was one that graced one of the first modern books on botanical discoveries. Garcia da Orta, a Portuguese doctor who was sent to Goa, spent part of his time describing the plants that he saw there after he arrived in 1534. His is one of the first great

Vasco da Gama died in Kochi on the west coast of India on his third voyage.
He was buried at the church now called St. Francis, but his remains
have been moved to Mosteiro dos Jerónimos west of Lisbon.

Black pepper, the fruit of a flowering vine native to the Malabar Coast, was
an enormously valuable trade good from the time of the Romans.
Garcia da Orta, a Portuguese physician and botanist, published
the first description of the plant.

works of botany of the Age of Exploration. Written in Portuguese, it was translated into Latin by Carolus Clusius, another trailblazing botanist. Europeans' wide-ranging travels during this period revealed a new world of plants and animals to the folks back home. Among other things, the spirit of scientific enquiry led to attempts to plant coveted flora in similar climates. In short order pepper was successfully transplanted to other areas in South India and South East Asia, but pepper from the Malabar Coast is still widely considered the best. The International Pepper Exchange is located on the other side of the Fort Kochi peninsula from St. Francis church. Pepper is not much used in local cuisine, however. The many varieties of that other pepper, *capsicum*, that originated in the Western Hemisphere, get pride of place in India today, in one of those gastronomic and horticultural exchanges that followed the great voyages of exploration.

The coast of Malabar was well known to the Romans, but Kochi as a port did not exist before 1341. That was when the River Periyar abruptly changed course, cutting a new channel through the backwaters, and leaving the former port closed off from the sea. The sudden shift in trading centers was due, in fact, to trade across the Indian Ocean. Arab mariners used mangrove trunks for the masts on their sailing vessels. Initially, mangroves in Oman were the major source, but demand eliminated the mangrove forests, and shipbuilders had to look elsewhere. The extensive groves on the Kerala coast were only a sail away, and soon they were being cut down. Today relatively few of the tangled forests survive, with severe consequences in terms of coastal erosion. Long stretches of sandy beach may attract vacationers, but they are prey to every storm that rushes in from the Arabian Sea. Along the beach at Fort Kochi big boulders have been piled up in an attempt to keep back the sea.

If you leave the seawall behind and walk to St. Francis church, you find that its white stucco façade and general style seem to have been inspired by a thousand churches built on the Iberian peninsula. It's unclear exactly what the church looked like in 1503 when the Portuguese built the first structure, however. It was part of the fort which the local Rajah permitted them to build at the mouth of the river as part of a trade agreement. Trunks of palm trees held together by iron bands appear to have been the major structural materials. A rampart of stone was built around the fort and the living quarters of the Portuguese. A few years later they received permission to build a larger church of mortar and stone. Completed in 1516, it was roofed with tiles, a major privilege since tile was reserved for palaces of local royalty and the temples where they worshipped.

By then the Portuguese had perfected their strategy of staging occasional battles and continuously conducting trade; within a few years the settlement at Kochi allowed them to control sea trade from Indonesia to Africa. One reason they chose Kochi was that they were barred from the more protected harbor at Goa, about 660 kilometers (410 miles) up the coast by the princeling in command there. He was in continual conflict with the Rajah of Cochin, who was pleased to give the foreigners a foothold, acting on the old "the enemy of my enemy is my friend" principle. It took two attacks on Goa before the authorities capitulated, and Goa became "Golden Goa," the Eastern jewel in the crown of Portuguese rulers. The Portuguese presence lasted until 1961 when the army of recently independent India invaded, ending more than 500 years of Portuguese control.

The Portuguese were lucky both in the timing of their arrival in the Indies and their determinion not to let initial difficulties hinder the accomplishment of their grand plans, says C. R. Boxer, the colorful historian who wrote widely about the Portuguese empire before his death at ninety-three in 2007. The refusal to accept defeat at Goa is an example of the way the Portuguese worked in the heady years after da Gama's first, world-changing voyage. They also suffered initial setbacks when they attacked two locations that remain strategic to this day: Ormuz, the island at the mouth of the Persian Gulf and Malacca, near the present Singapore, guarding the straits leading to the South China Sea. From each defeat they came back with greater force and better strategy.

The first Portuguese viceroy was able to destroy what Boxer calls "a makeshift" fleet from Egypt and part of India a little north of Goa in 1509, thus "eliminating the only Muslim naval force capable of meeting the Portuguese warships on something approaching equal terms." At the time Shia and Sunni Muslim rulers were squaring off to fight each other over which group truly followed the Prophet's tradition, and were therefore unable or uninterested in rebuilding the fleet. Another bit of luck for the Portuguese was that Hindu merchants had no interest in

Goa (detail) as depicted by Jan Huyghen van Linschoten, the Dutch traveler
and historian who traveled to the Estado da Índia in 1583.

seafaring—high caste Brahmins considered a sea voyage defiling—and
so did not step in to fill the gap. By playing one local group off against
another, the Portuguese ruled the seas, allowing ships they licensed to
travel, but feeling free to attack and capture the cargoes of any ship
they didn't.

But these lucky circumstances pale compared to the fortuitous
timing whose traces can still be seen near the entrance to the mouth of
the Kochi harbor. The Chinese fishing nets there are now as much a
tourist attraction as St. Francis Church. Their gossamer-like mesh is
lowered at low tide into the sea water from graceful, arching supports
and then winched out at high tide. The fisher folk hope that the nets
will be full of the bounty of the sea, while local commerce hopes for the
bounty of the tourist. Standard postcard photos of the sun setting gor-

geously behind the nets or of rugged fishermen sell briskly, while guided tours usually include a stop for visitors to take their own pictures.

How long ago the nets were originally installed is unclear, although they date from before the visits of great Chinese treasure fleet. Had the Portuguese discovered the *volta do mar* at beginning of the fifteenth century instead of the end, they might have encountered the Chinese when they rounded the tip of Africa. The Ming dynasty sent out seven waves of ships, beginning in 1407 and ending in 1434. The huge flotillas of 150 ships or more carried treasure to distribute wherever the fleet called. The usual commercial motivation seemed in this case to take a back seat to a desire to impress and to receive homage from societies that the Chinese considered backward if not barbarian. The fleet made it to the east coast of Africa and possibly sailed as far as Australia. They stopped on the Malabar Coast at least three times. The Chinese admiral considered the rulers at Kochi a cut above those elsewhere in India.

In the 1420s the policy changed with a change in emperor; the last voyage set out in 1426 and returned home 1434. Besides the treasure ships, the Ming dynasty navy at its height consisted of 3,500 vessels: 2,700 warships and dozens of patrol stations up and down the Chinese coast, 400 near Nanjin, and 400 armed transport vessels for grain. Compared to the size and wealth of the Chinese flotilla, the Portuguese effort appears puny. But the Chinese had ended their adventure when the Portuguese began theirs, so the coast was literally clear for them.

On Vasco da Gama's last trip to India, in 1524, he came down with malaria, and died on Christmas Day. The current St. Francis Church has a plaque marking the spot where he was buried. His body rested there for fourteen years; then it was disinterred and shipped back to Portugal. It was reburied on the estate that the king had awarded him after his first trips, but his remains were removed to the magnificent Mosteiro, designed in part as a monument to his accomplishment, when it was completed.

But it's that first voyage of Vasco da Gama that everyone remembers. It was a signal accomplishment and became the centerpiece in the defining work of Portuguese literature, the epic poem *The Lusiads*.

There must be a connection between the way three great world-exploring powers of the late Renaissance produced their most celebrated writers within the same span of a few decades. William Shakespeare

(1564-1616), Miguel de Cervantes (1547-1616) and Luís Vaz de Camões (1524?-1580) were roughly contemporaries, with Cervantes and Shakespeare actually dying on the same day, April 23, 1616. The literary forms they chose to express their view of the world were different: Shakespeare was an actor turned playwright, Cervantes wrote poetry and novels while making a living as a slightly disreputable tax collector, and Camões was a man-at-arms who spent fourteen years in India before publishing his long poem. The societies they lived in were in exuberant expansion, with tidings from new worlds arriving regularly. Each writer can be said to have contributed enormously to the development of the language their people used.

Camões thought he was working in a classic form when he began *The Lusiads* with an echo of *The Aeneid*. He aimed to create an epic that would glorify the Portuguese the way Virgil glorified the Romans. But unlike Virgil, he sings of "arms and the illustrious men" not of "arms and of a man" and therein lies an important difference. Camões gives da Gama long speeches where he explains not only the challenges of his first expedition to India, but also the whole of Portuguese history. The kings and heroes who formed Portugal are showered with praise and are, Camões proclaims, beloved of the gods. The simple sailors are also men whom the gods cherish, receiving at the end of the epic a mythic reward. On the way home, they visit an island where they enjoy an idyll with gorgeous nymphs, partaking of some of the most explicit sex recorded in classic literature. So suggestive is the verse that during the prudish twentieth-century dictatorship of António Salazar that section of the epic was removed from all editions even though the poem was a standard text in Portuguese schools. This led, of course, to copies of the section alone being circulated and read avidly by adolescents who may have paid more attention to it than they did to the rest of poem.

The epic tells about the glories and the difficulties of the Portuguese adventure. Camões knew firsthand how hard the life of a sailor was. Not only was food monotonous and frequently moldy, instead of keeping the men healthy, it actually contributed to their death, particularly on long voyages. The culprit was the lack of Vitamin C in the standard rations which included very little fruit and vegetables on long voyages and which gave rise to scurvy. (The cause-and-effect connection between diet and scurvy took a long time to be understood. It was the mid-eighteenth century before a British naval surgeon tested the idea that limes and oranges would make a difference).

Scurvy seems not to have presented problems during the first decades of Portuguese exploration along the coast of Africa. Ships put in frequently at islands or sheltered bays to take on water and supplies including local fruits. But once seafarers stayed at sea for months at a time, problems developed. Vasco da Gama lost two-thirds of his men to scurvy, and Camões, who made the trip to India and back twice, knew what he was describing in *The Lusiads*. He has Vasco da Gama say that among the worst challenges the mariners faced was the disease which rendered, "Ghastly the mouth and gums enormous swell'd;/… putrid like a dead man's wound,(It) Poisoned with foetid streams the air round./ … [E]ach dreamy mournful hour we gave/Some brave companion to a foreign grave."

Camões describes the glorious deaths of Portugal's heroes in events beginning with the fight to expel the Moors until some sixty-five years after Vasco da Gama's voyage. Death from scurvy is far from glorious, however; perhaps this is why Camões gives Vasco da Gama's crew that imaginary idyll on the way back. The visit to an enchanted island arranged by the gods is extremely different from what actually occurred—the death of half the crew and months of fighting the winds off the east coast of Africa because they left when unfavorable monsoon winds were blowing. Significantly, Camões begins his account of this stop-over with a description of "limpid streams" and of the fruit trees that cover the island. He mentions oranges, citrons and lemons ("molded like a maiden's breasts"), then lists cherries, mulberries, peaches, pomegranates, grapes and pears, as if the first thing on the sailors' minds was just exactly what they needed to regain their health. His description of the flirtatious nymphs and the quite explicit sex they engage in with the sailors follows. (Perhaps it's worth noting that Vasco da Gama was not married when he went on this first voyage. On his return he married a well-born woman and had half a dozen children with her.)

One way of reading *The Lusiads* is to understand it as a memorial to the past of the Portuguese empire, even though at the time of its creation, the empire's future seemed bright. Camões ends his epic by glorifying the young king Sebastião, who had just ascended the throne. Handsome and bright, Sebastião was convinced that his destiny was to continue the conquest of Moorish lands and to follow the example of his ancestors by invading North Africa. No matter that the last attempt, led by Sebastião's great-great granduncle Henrique in 1437, had ended in disaster. But Sebastião's attempt to take Tangier also ended in a debacle. His body was never found; this led his followers to pray for his return as a Messiah. In the meantime, a successor had to be found. Sebastião had not yet married and left no child. The crown passed to the next in line, another Henrique, a cardinal who was Sebastião's uncle. When he died, the winner among the royals competing for the Portuguese crown was Phillip II of Spain, who ruled as Filipe I of Portugal.

There followed a sixty-year period when Portuguese mariners sailed under the Spanish flag. Juan Rodriguez Cabrillo (named João Rodrigues Cabrilho at birth) explored the west coast of North America, charting San Diego harbor and the Gulf of California. There's a statue of Cabrillo on Point Loma at the Cabrillo National Monument, not far from the Fernandes family's grocery store that made such a deep impression on me as a child.

Before that temporary eclipse of Portuguese power, however, they pushed farther east toward the rich islands of the southwest Pacific. Less than fifteen years after Vasco da Gama's triumphal return, the Portuguese controlled Malacca, where the Malay peninsula is separated from the island of Sumatra by less than two kilometers (1.25 miles). The narrow Straits of Malacca provided the most direct route from the Indian Ocean to the South China Sea and the Pacific Ocean, to the farther Spice Islands and beyond to China and Japan. Their strategic importance continues; more tonnage passes through them yearly than through any other sea lane.

Malacca was primarily a beachhead from which further sorties could be launched. Afonso de Albuquerque, the viceroy, intended to capture the islands of Banda and Maluku, which were the only places where nutmeg, mace and cloves grew. By 1522 the Portuguese had built a fortress on Ternate, an island 4,000 kilometers (2,500 miles) east of Malacca at the doorway to the Pacific. By mid-century they had established the emporium of Macau, that enclave on the mainland of China which would remain the last colony in Portuguese hands until 1999, when it was turned over to China, two years after the British relinquished control of Hong Kong. In 1571 the Portuguese took a foothold in Japan with the establishment of Nagasaki, which also became the center of Jesuit missionary activity in the region.

Among the crew members on these early voyages was Fernão de Maghelhães (a.k.a. Ferdinand Magellan) who would later sail for Spain, attempting to follow Columbus's lead and visit the Spice Islands by going west. His expedition successfully circumnavigated the globe (eighteen members of his crew made it back) but he was killed in the Philippines. The islands—named after the Spanish king Philip II, by then also king of Portugal—subsequently became colonies of Spain governed from Mexico. Under the Treaty of Tordesillas, signed in 1494 and amended in 1529, Spain had papal approval to claim all territory west of a meridian now figured to be about forty-five degrees west, which runs for the most part through the Atlantic Ocean. Portugal had dibs on the land to the east, which has come to include Brazil: Rio is located about forty-three degrees west longitude. On the other side of the world their spheres of influence met again, with Spain getting most of the Pacific Ocean.

By the late seventeenth century, the Dutch supplanted Portugal in much of its eastern territory. The Dutch even took over the outpost at Nagasaki in Japan. But the Portuguese presence in its former colonies has proved to be far more long-lasting than this early hand-off of territory would suggest. Part of the influence is due to the missionary efforts of the Catholic Church which began almost with the first Portuguese ships to arrive in the Spice Islands. Part of it is also the result of the attitude of the Portuguese toward local women. The Dutch alienated local populations by practicing "ethnic cleansing" in places they wanted to control or whose monopoly on a spice they wanted to destroy. The most flagrant case was on Niera, one of the Banda Islands (now part of Indonesia) and one of the few places where nutmeg grew. In order to control the production of the spice, several thousand Bandanese were killed and the rest enslaved in the 1620s. Resentment over this simmers to this day. The Portuguese, on the other hand, rarely massacred locals, although they might use them as slaves. And wherever the caravels went they were more likely to make love than war. Therein lies the reason for much of the Portuguese influence around the world (there will be more about the sex life of an empire in a later chapter).

Language is a kind of shadow cast on the earth by a powerful country. These days when people count the speakers of languages, Mandarin Chinese comes out on top no matter who does the counting, but there is much inconsistency further down the list. Portuguese is number six on several lists. French sometimes makes the top dozen, but Dutch never rates higher than about forty-fifth.

The Portuguese did not appreciate the complexities of the religions practiced by populations in the areas they were attempting to control. However, their success was facilitated by differences between religions they had encountered before, albeit in different forms from those they found in the Estado da Índia. For example, it is doubtful that the Portuguese understood that the Muslims they were up against in India or in the Spice Islands were different from those who had been expelled from Portugal in the twelfth century. Certainly, the word they used to describe the Muslims they encountered was *Mauro*, or Moors, which strictly speaking should refer to the Arabs from the Middle East and North Africa who swept northward into Europe in the eighth and ninth centuries. But the Islam of these Far Eastern regions had been spread much more peacefully. Muslim traders and mariners frequently established families at the ports they visited—taking more than one wife (provided you treat them all equally) is perfectly legitimate in Islam. The children of these unions were raised as Muslims largely without the heritage of religious warfare.

Furthermore, there are at least three great strands of Islam, the Sunni, Shia and Sufi. The Sufi strand has historically been less austere than the others. It arrived in the great archipelago that now forms the nation of Indonesia, and on the islands farther to the east, not long before the Portuguese did. Indeed, on many islands Islam was introduced by Chinese mariners who were part of the Ming dynasty's Treasure Fleet of the early fifteenth century. Since Islam was not as deeply entrenched there as it was around the Mediterranean, the struggle for souls undertaken by the missionaries who traveled with the Portuguese may have been easier.

Francis Xavier, one of the pillars of the Society of Jesus, reached the west coat of India in 1542. In ten years he traveled, preached and converted from Goa through Malacca as far as the Spice Islands and up to Japan before dying on an island off the coast of China. His memory looms in the history of Christian missionary work, and without a doubt he left a legacy of converts throughout the Estado da Índia. But the Christianity he preached was only the most recent version of the religion of Jesus Christ to have reached India.

When Vasco da Gama arrived in what is now southern India the region already had a long history with Judaism, Christianity and Islam. Jews arrived on the Malabar coast in the diaspora after the fall of the Second Temple in 52 BC. A group of local Christians claims a connection to Jesus that goes back to shortly after the crucifixion. Just as the remains of St. James supposedly made their way through the Straits of Gibraltar and around to Campostella on the Atlantic coast of Spain, so St. Thomas the Apostle was said to have set off after the death of Christ to evangelize in the East, making it all the way to India. A Christian community in India is documented as far back as the fourth century, while news of a tomb of St. Thomas containing his relics in southern India reached Rome before 590. The Christians in Kerala received official recognition from Cheraman Perumal, the king of Malabar, some forty years later; the leader was interested in foreign beliefs; and is supposed to have converted to Islam from Hinduism three years before the death of the Prophet Mohammed in 632. In the middle of the ninth century the South-Indian Christian community was strengthened by contacts with Christians in Syria, which developed into official recognition by the Patriarch of Antioch.

But the Christianity practiced was not the sort of Christianity that Francis Xavier recognized. Although Roman Catholicism arrived with the Portuguese, it was soon clear to the ecclesiastical authorities that there was much to be done if the work of bringing the True Church to the unenlightened was to go forward. The Portuguese king requested the help of Ignatius Loyola and the newly founded Jesuit order, with the result that Francis Xavier left Lisbon on April 7, 1541. It was a departure late in the year, both for the *volta do mar* and the crossing of the Indian Ocean on monsoon winds, and Xavier did not arrive in Goa until more than a year later, May 6, 1542. Initially he thought that Goa was completely populated by Christians, but he became discouraged at the actual level of religious practice on the part of both Portuguese and converts.

This missionary effort was conducted against a backdrop of the great religious changes which were going on in Europe. In October 1517

Martin Luther nailed his Ninety-five Theses to a church door, marking the beginning of the grand Reformation of western Christianity. The conduct of the Roman Catholic Church was undergoing serious questioning. A mass of contradictions had developed within the church: remember that in 1383 King João I of Portugal, despite the fact that he had d been in a quasi-military religious order, fathered three children before he formally asked permission to break his vow of chastity so he could marry Philippa of Lancaster. A century and a half later when Ignatius Loyola founded the Company of Jesus along military lines this kind of thing was no longer allowed.

This was not a quarrel with another faith, but within the larger Christian one. The holy book of Catholics and Protestants was basically the same document (with a few more sections among the Catholics than among the Protestants) and they all believed that Jesus Christ was the Son of God who came to earth to redeem humanity. The differences can be seen as simply nuances in that belief, but, as is clear from any study of religion, the small things can be the most cutting. Among Christians, the question of whether the wine and bread in the communion become literally or figuratively the body and blood of Christ lay behind the killing of thousands.

The reforming zeal inside the Catholic Church meant that new energy was poured into devotions—this was the age of mystics like St. John of the Cross and St. Teresa of Avila—and into making sure that other Christians did not backslide. In Portugal, Italy and Spain the chief means of doing this was the Inquisition, begun in Spain in 1481 and in Portugal in 1531, and the Jesuits in the Estado da Índia were proud to carry this on.

There were four offices of the Inquisition in Portugal: in Lisbon, Évora, Porto and Goa. At the beginning, the main thrust of their concern was whether or not Catholics followed the tenets of their faith as they should. In Spain people suspected of bigamy and blasphemy were vigorously pursued, but in relatively short order, the Inquisition in Portugal placed emphasis on investigating the way in which converts from Judaism (and Islam to a lesser extent) lived as good Christians. This became a double bind: Jews and Muslims had been expelled from Spain in 1492 by the very Catholic rulers, Ferdinand and Isabella, in order to "cleanse" their kingdoms. Many thousands had taken refuge in

Portugal, among them was the father of the doctor-botanist Garcia da Orta whose book on the plants of India was so celebrated. The persecution of Jews was nothing new in Europe. They were expelled from England in 1290 and from France in 1306, while there were frequent pogroms during the fourteenth century in the Spanish kingdoms, including mass killings in 1391 with forced conversions.

After an initial welcome, Jews in Portugal at the turn of the sixteenth century were forced to convert, leave the country or be executed. Thousands were killed; estimates vary but it is thought that between 1,000 and 4,000 were burned in Lisbon in the spring of 1506. The majority converted, many through coercion, becoming *novos cristões,* or New Christians. For a while they were allowed to live in peace, with many becoming important members of the community. In 1558, the Portuguese Inquisition—because it had run out of work rooting out slack religious practice elsewhere, one historian suggests—turned to the converted Jews, looking for lapses in Christian practice or signs of secretly held Jewish sympathies. The delicious pork and clam stew, *Porco á Alentejana,* has its origins in one of the tests given New Christians to see if they had renounced Judaism and its rules against eating pork and shellfish. The result of this harassment was the migration of many Jews and New Christians to other countries, notably the Netherlands, but also a large movement of New Christians to Brazil and other frontiers of the Portuguese empire. This included the Estado da Índia: in 1565 the Rajah of Cochin gave Jews fleeing persecution permission to build a synagogue next to his own temple. (Garcia da Orta was still alive, but by then he had moved to what is now Mumbai, a city whose sprawling form still bears witness to the two centuries it prospered as a Portuguese trading center.)

The sincerity of many of the converts from Judaism was above reproach, and certainly their children, reared as Catholics, frequently became extremely dedicated Christians. St. Teresa, for example, was the daughter of a converted Spanish Jew, while Diego de Laínez, one of St. Ignatius Loyola's colleagues in the founding of the Jesuits, was the son of one. But through a horrendous excess of zeal, hundreds were killed in Portugal and abroad, among them the sister of Garcia da Orta who had moved to India and was burned at the stake in 1569. He had died the year before of natural causes, but in 1580 his body was ordered exhumed from its grave in a Catholic cemetery on the Indian coast, and his bones burned.

His book, one of the first to be published in Goa, survived. The Latin translation by Clusius was much abridged, focusing on the botanical information, replacing the original elegant woodcuts with later ones, and leaving out the dialogues between da Orta and a friend, that give glimpses of what the country and society was like in this far outpost of the Lusitanians. An English translation was published in 1913, made from a copy of the original book found in the Bodleian library. That version is available in some libraries, but frequently only to researchers who must wear white gloves to turn the pages. And, while an Indian publisher reprinted it twenty years ago, few copies of that edition made it out of South Asia. It is a pity that it is not more widely available, if only to read in da Orta's own words his attitude toward Judaism: "a false faith" he writes more than once. Or to see the reproduction of the poem that Camões wrote to him, playing on da Orta's name (which means "garden" in Portuguese), to thank him for providing him with a place in which to grow his poetry. It would appear that Portugal's bard used da Orta's library to research Portuguese history as he worked on his great epic poem during the long years he passed in the Estado da Índia.

There are only a handful of Jews in Cochin today, although for hundreds of years it was a thriving center of Jewish life. Kerala had several synagogues, and two distinct groups of Jews—Black Jews from the original group, there since the beginning of the Common Era, and White Jews, immigrants from Europe and the Middle East after the persecutions of the sixteenth through eighteenth centuries. After India's independence and the establishment of the state of Israel at the end of the 1940s, however, the community dwindled rapidly. The Pardesi synagogue is the only one of seven synagogues to remain open. For a few hours most mornings and afternoons, visitors can admire its floor made of seventeenth century blue and white tiles imported from China, its chandeliers of Belgian crystal, and its Torah bedecked with gold and silver ornaments, some of which were given to the community by the local Rajah. But Friday night prayers are sometimes now delayed for hours as the faithful wait for the arrival of the tenth man—who may be an American backpacker or an Israeli businessman passing through by chance—to form the *minyan* necessary to start the service.

St. Francis Church in Kochi is also still a functioning place of worship, although far removed from its origins as a Roman Catholic institution on what was then, the far fringes of the expanding Portuguese empire. Originally it was called Igreja de Santo Antonio, and was administered by the Franciscans. When the Dutch took over the coast in 1663, they expropriated it for their own Reformed Church. The Roman Catholic altar and screens were removed to a church on the other side of Lake Vembanad which was the only Catholic church allowed to continue to function by the Protestant Dutch. When the British arrived on the scene in 1795, they refurbished the building which had fallen to ruin. It was apparently at this time that it was renamed, the Church of St. Francis, with no connection to the Jesuit missionary who epitomized the fervor of a Church desiring to convert millions.

It has been more than sixty years since Goa became part of India, and the last official link between Portugal and the Estado da Índia was broken. St. Francis Church now belongs to the Church of South India, a denomination in the Anglican Communion founded in 1947 when India became independent. Nevertheless evidence of Portugal's long association remains on India's western coast, in material things like architecture and also in cultural things like names. Rodrigues, Moniz, da Costa, Saldhana, Gomes and others—you'll find them in nearly every town along the coast, reminders of the intimate relation between Portugal, the Portuguese and the people of the countries where they traveled.

CHAPTER FOUR

Slavery

"PETER GOMES" IS A NAME you'll find in Goa. One was a well-known composer and performer of musical plays in the Konkani language, called *tiatr* from the Portuguese word for theatre. You'll find the name in Canada, where Peter Gomes, also born in Goa, is a piano tuner in British Columbia. There are Pedro Gomeses in Africa today. One was a member of Angola's indoor soccer team in at the 2006 Lusaphone games when the team had a 2-2 record in the competition. Another Pedro Gomes was governor of the Brazilian province of Rio de Janeiro in 1681, while Pedro Gomes Pereira was a governor of Angola in the seventeenth century.

It should be no surprise that there are several Peter Gomeses in the United States too. What is a surprise is that one of them, the esteemed African-American theologian and Harvard professor Peter Gomes, is not nearly as African as he thought and that an analysis of his DNA indicates just how far-reaching the Portuguese adventure goes. Gomes, whose father came from the Cape Verde islands and whose mother's family from the American South, was one of twelve African Americans featured in the PBS series *African American Lives 2*. DNA analysis shows that not only is Gomes about one-third European, but also that one of his ancestors was a Jewish man who probably arrived in the Cape Verde islands after leaving Portugal sometime around 1529, just a few years before Garcia da Orta set out for India. "Well," Gomes told executive producer Henry L. Gates, Jr., when the analysis was presented to him, "any family worth belonging to has a Jew in it somewhere or other."

Gomes' story says a lot about what has happened in Africa during the last 550 years. The Cape Verde islands were not inhabited when Alvise de Cadamosto, an Italian mariner working under Infante Henrique's orders, discovered them in the mid-1400s as the Portuguese worked their way down the west coast of Africa, exploring sea lanes which no one had travelled before. Foremost in their minds was the quest for the source of African gold and for a route to the wealth of the Indies, but—along with a mission to convert the heathen—they also were interested in slaves.

Slavery was nothing new. Learned Greek slaves educated Romans, the war ships of antiquity were rowed by galley slaves, the Hebrews of the Old Testament were slaves in Egypt and Babylon, our English word slave has its root in the servitude of Slavonic people after their conquest by Otto the Great in the tenth century. In feudal times, the status of a serf or vassal was not much different from that of a slave in the sense that they could be sold along with land. But by the beginning of the Renaissance, slavery had become a marginal practice in Northern Europe, largely because of the kind of crops and economic arrangements there. On the borderlands of Europe, however, the institution continued, with Christian slaves in Algiers and Muslim ones in Seville and Cordoba.

Slaves from south of the Sahara reached the Mediterranean in the same caravans that carried gold and ivory to the ports of the Maghreb, like Ceuta. Some of them were far from being the sad, terribly treated creatures who would become the norm later on. The Russian poet Alexander Pushkin was the grandson of a man from an African royal family (sometimes recorded as being from Chad, sometimes Abyssinia), who was captured, sent to the Turkish capital of Constantinople in the mid-eighteenth century, and then sold to the Russian Tsar. His elite status was recognized from the beginning; he was sent to France for military training and ended up marrying into a wealthy land-owning family. Among other notable African-Europeans are the French novelist Alexandre Dumas (his father was the son of a slave and a French landowner in what is now Haiti) and George Polgreen Bridgewater, one of Beethoven's favorite violinists who gave the first performance of the Kreutzer Sonata, with Beethoven playing the piano part.

The most illustrious case of a slave leaving upper-class descendants, however, is that of one of the mistresses of Portugal's fifth king, Afonso III, who reigned in the thirteenth century. She was a slave and may or may not have been African—one early source says she was Moor, which frequently meant a mixed-race African. Her descendants married up: her great-great-great-great-great-granddaughter Charlotte married

George III of England, and Charlotte's "Negroid" features were remarked upon during her lifetime.

All of these cases are starkly different from those of members of the North American elite who had long-term sexual relations with slaves. The children American President Thomas Jefferson had with his slave Sally Hemings, for example, received training as artisans, but none of them slipped into America's upper class.

There are at least three reasons for this. First was the nature of slavery in Africa itself, particularly when the slave trade began in earnest. According to historian John Thornton, slavery on much of the continent was considerably different from slavery as known in Europe or as it developed in the New World. Yes, people could be bought and sold, but their status, contemporary observers noted, was not particularly dishonorable. Because land in much of Africa could not be owned by individuals, owning slaves meant owning the source of wealth the way owning land in Europe did. Indeed, Thornton compares some West African conflicts which ended in the capture of slaves to the wars of Medieval and Renaissance European states and principalities over the land and the wealth that could derived there from. It was in the owner's interest to see that slaves were treated well enough to be productive, he states. Frequently they were skilled in such things as metalworking or served as managers, keeping part of the profit from their work. From the time of the arrival of European adventurers African kings had no qualms about selling slaves to the Portuguese and others because the institution was so familiar.

Some slaves who were taken captive in wars had been members of their society's elite before their enslavement, and they were frequently recognized as such by those who owned them. Being enslaved was a personal tragedy for a prince of the Joloffs of the region where Pushkin's ancestor came from, but a high-born African's qualities—his skill with horses, his literacy (in Arabic, to be sure) and his manner of being accustomed to deference, perhaps—would be familiar to European nobles. A slave from the higher classes of his (or her) home society would also be an exotic luxury in the fourteenth through mid-seventeenth century and might be treated well the way a fine horse would be. The result was that some high-born African slaves entered rather easily into elite society.

Conversion to Catholicism continued to be a major motivation for Portuguese expeditions. Several popes blessed wars aimed at converting Jews and Muslims. From there it was no stretch to bless conversion of pagans: one argument in favor of slavery held that it was better for an African to be baptized even if he or she might suffer in slavery than to die at home a heathen. To most twenty-first century ears this may sound twisted, but it includes recognition on the part of Catholic clergy and laymen that Africans were human beings, a concept that wasn't always present in colonial empires.

When Portuguese sailors and explorers had children with local women, they were claimed by the church and baptized even when their parents weren't married. Today's multiracial Portuguese-speaking societies found everywhere the Portuguese went are as tangible a reminder of the Portuguese adventure as are the *padrões*, those columns of stone which they carried with them and inscribed with the names of voyagers and the dates of landings.

The first voyages down the coast of Africa brought the Portuguese neither converts nor wealth, however. The northwest coast is dry, with the Sahara Desert coming right down to the sea. Cabo Bojador, the legendary promontory which stopped all exploration for centuries, is no more than a collection of dunes and rocks emerging from the desert. Viewed today from the air, it is hard to understand how the cape, whose name in Arabic, *Abu Khatar*, means "the father of danger," could have kept navigators from going farther south for so long. Yet recent sailing instructions suggest that the low coastline looks deceptively innocent; they warn that the depths shift almost capriciously, the winds switch here to blow in all seasons from the northeast, while the current rushing southward is strong. Sailors accustomed to sailing within the sight of land might panic at the thought of being swept out to sea, since the idea of the *volta do mar* would not be developed for decades.

Once Cabo Bojador is rounded, the coastline appears uninviting for hundreds of kilometers south. Cadamosto does not mention in his accounts any prominent features from Cabo Branco (white cape), on what is now the northern border between Mauritania and Western Sahara, to the island of Arguin, on the southern border of Mauritania and Senegal. Arguin had good springs to replenish ships' water supplies.

It would become a major trans-shipment point for the slave trade, but on the first exploratory voyages it was uninhabited. It wasn't until Cadamosto's expedition approached the Senegal River that they began to encounter many people.

Their large sailing vessels impressed the Africans who used dugout canoes for fishing, but the people on the West African coast had not discovered sails. Cadamosto reports that many took their ships

for large birds with white wings ... and when the sails were furled, they conjectured, from their length, and swimming on the water, that they must be great fish. Others again believed that they were spirits, who wandered about by night; because they were seen at anchor in the evening at one place, and would be seen next morning 100 miles off, either proceeding along the coast to the southwards, or put back, according as the wind changed, or the caravels might happen to steer. They could not conceive how human beings could travel more in one night than they were able to perform themselves in three days; by which they were confirmed in the notion of the ships being spirits.

He adds that they thought the portholes in the stern were

real eyes, by which the vessel was able to find her way in the sea; and observed that travelers on land found difficulty to find the road from one place to another, while we were able to travel along the trackless ocean; and that the whites must therefore be the greatest of sorcerers, not inferior to the devil himself.

Only one group of Africans that Cadamosto and his ships encountered on that first voyage was unfriendly. Fifteen canoes or *almadias,* each with eight to ten men, came out to challenge the ships. That skirmish near the Gambia River was enough to persuade the crewmen to insist that the expedition turn back.

At this point they were near the most westerly point in the shoulder of the continent and not far from the Cape Verde islands, which take their name from the tree-covered highland near present-day Dakar.

Subsequent expeditions would find the coastline veering to the south and east, initially giving rise to hopes that the route to the Indies would be short, or that one of the great rivers which flowed out of the mainland might connect with the Nile and the kingdom of the legendary Prester John, or that they might be the rivers the Bible says flow out of Eden.

The rivers did lead into the heart of the continent, but not to Paradise. The Senegal was navigable for 830 kilometers (580 miles) of its long, looping trajectory. The Portuguese ships could sail more than 320 kilometers (200 miles) up the Gambia. Relatively little settlement lay along the coast, and the trade routes led inland to meet the caravan routes which circled throughout the interior of West Africa, leading north toward the Mediterranean. Because of the long distances and difficult terrain, only high-value items were transported. Slaves not only fetched good prices at the end of the route, but they could also be used to transport gold and ivory. The fact that salt, mined in the middle of the Sahara from the residue of ancient inland seas, was a major trade good going south says a great deal about where settlements were located. East African coastal communities frequently make their own salt, but this was rare on the Western coast.

Cadamosto confirms that on the west coast, the locals "seldom go out to sea, or to any distance from their own coasts, lest they should be taken by their neighbors and sold for slaves." He adds that the highly placed men of the country of the Senegal had no great wealth or lands in the European sense, but they were attended by immense retinues of servants, many of whom were slaves.

It is against this backdrop that trade in African slaves began. The first shipment preceded Cadamosto's trip by four years when two Portuguese captains took twelve Africans from Cabo Branco to Portugal as slaves in 1441. Three years later a shipment of 263 slaves from Africa arrived in Portugal. Infante Henrique, who got a fifth of the proceeds from their sale, ordered a grand celebration welcoming them. It was a heartbreaking sight for Gomes Eanes de Zurara, an official royal chronicler:

> (What) heart, however, hardened it might be, could not be
> pierced by a feeling of pity at the sight of that company? Some
> held their heads low, their faces bathed in tears as they looked

at each other; some groaned very piteously, looking towards the heavens fixedly and crying out aloud, as if they were calling on the father of the universe to help them; others struck their faces with their hands and threw themselves full length on the ground; yet others lamented in the form of a chant, according to the custom of their naïve land, and though the words of the language in which they sang could not be understood by our people, the chant revealed clearly enough the degree of their grief. To increase their anguish still more, those who had charge of the division then arrived and began to separate them one from another so they formed five equal lots. This made it necessary to separate sons from their fathers and wives from their husbands and brother from brother. No account was taken of friendship or relationship, each ending up wherever chance placed him. …Who could carry out such a division without great difficulty for as soon as the children who had been assigned to one group saw their parents in another they jumped up and ran towards them; mothers clasped their other children in their arms and lay face downwards on the ground, accepting wounds with contempt for the suffering of their flesh rather than let their children be torn from them.

Despite such tragic scenes, the sale opened the doors to the slave trade. Until that point only fifty-one ships had ever set sail from Portugal for the African coast, but in 1446 alone twenty-six ships pursued the African trade. Papal bulls in 1452 and 1454 gave Portugal permission to reduce any non-Christians to slaves and gave the Portuguese a monopoly on trade of all sorts with Africa. Skirmishes in the Maghreb and along the border with Spain after Infante Henrique's death in 1460 slowed the pace of exploration for two decades. When João II became king in 1481, attention turned to pushing farther and farther down the coast with the twin aims of finding riches and saving souls. In 1482 the Portuguese established a trading center, church and fortress at Elmina on what was then called the Gold Coast, now Ghana. They hoped to make it a center for trading for gold. It was mined in small operations at many places in the interior, but the precious metal never became as profitable as the slave trade.

In 1482, Diogo Cão and his ships came upon the Congo River, a huge watercourse sending a plume of fresh water and detritus from the continent miles into the ocean. Cão's reports to the king prompted a second expedition a year later. A small flotilla loaded with trade goods, missionaries and tradesmen with their families set out to trade, convert the natives and build a church fitting for a Catholic country. (It should be noted that the wives and daughters of the masons and carpenters were among the rare women to take part in such a venture. at any point in the Portuguese adventure. The Spanish consistently sent out far more women than the Portuguese did, which had profound effects on the way the two colonial empires developed. By the 1590s, a third of the passengers in outward-bound Spanish ships were females, a figure only attained in Portuguese immigration in the nineteenth century when family groups were recruited to work on coffee plantations in Brazil.)

The caravels of this second expedition navigated several kilometers upstream along the Congo River, at times ten kilometers (6.25 miles wide), before they encountered the forward posts of the kingdom

São Jorge da Mina was founded as a Portuguese slave trading station in 1482 in what is now Ghana. The country's old name, the Gold Coast, refers to the riches found in the interior: Africans who had worked in the mines there became prized slaves when gold and diamond mining began in Brazil in the eighteenth century.

of Kongo. People "of a favorable aspect" came down to the river to greet them. The capital, Mbanza Kongo, was on a table land 300 kilometers (190 miles) away. Called São Salvador in Portuguese times, it lies inside the current boundaries of Angola and has readopted its former name. Cão decided to send the missionaries there, guided by the welcoming committee of locals. They journeyed on foot for twenty days and reported that the city was about the size of Évora in Portugal, with a population about 15,000. Its altitude meant it was less hot than the coast; because of the heat and insects, Cão and his colleagues found it insufferable to wait there for the overland party's return. Instead they put out to sea to explore a bit further south.

What followed was a meeting of cultures which was far from unequal. Indeed, as historian John Thornton emphasizes, the African societies were advanced. For example, iron production in sub-Saharan Africa dates back to at least 600 BCE, and because of the scarcity of fuel, ironworkers developed a way of superheating the air for the smelting process that is very much like the blast furnace technology of nineteenth century Europe. Africans produced "amazingly good-quality steel—perhaps the best steel in the world of the time, and certainly equal to or even better than the steel produced in early modern Europe."

Textile production was both skilled and abundant. The Mandingo people of Mali made a kind of velvet from pounded bark that amazed the Europeans, who also noted the quality of the cotton cloth used throughout much of West Africa. In Kongo, cloth woven from the fibers of the raffia palm was comparable to plush and satin. From statistics kept by the Portuguese after they took control of trade on the coast, Thornton concludes that cloth production in the kingdom of Kongo was on a par with that of the great textile-producing areas of Northern Europe. In 1611, for example, he notes that 100,000 meters (109,000 yards) of cloth produced in Kongo (population about 150,000) were exported to the neighboring territory of Angola, which compares with the amount of cloth produced in the Dutch city of Leiden, whose population was about the same.

Food production was more than sufficient to support a well-nourished population. Crops included yams, rice and various kinds of edible palms which grow well where rains come during the warm season and day-length varies little. Bananas and taro were also widely cultivated.

Farther north where conditions were dryer, millet and sorghum were basic crops. This means, Thornton says, that the Africans had no need to trade with the Europeans for basic commodities. Like the upper classes of Europe who sought spices, gold and silks, the Africans wanted luxuries—horses, textiles they weren't familiar with, jewelry and the like. A relatively small amount of unworked copper and iron and some finished metal goods were also in demand, but that added up to only about ten percent of the estimated actual need for replacement metal.

The culture that the Portuguese encountered in the Congo basin during the fifteenth century was ready to take what it found interesting from the Europeans, but did not consider itself inferior in any way. The king was not pleased when Cão weighed anchor with four highly placed members of his court on board. He threatened to kill the missionaries who stayed behind if Cão did not return in fifteen months. When the ships did return with gifts and the news that the Portuguese royal family had sponsored the baptism of the kidnapped Congolese, the missionaries had more success in converting the king and his court.

Thus began one of the longest colonial relations between Africans and Europeans, lasting nearly 500 years. The end came with the peaceful revolution in 1974 in the mother country. It was led by armed forces officers disgusted by the way Portugal's civilian leadership insisted on holding onto the African colonies through a grueling colonial war.

Millions of slaves were shipped through the Angolan port of Luanda, as well as the other slave trading centers of Elmina, Sierra Leone and Arguin. The authorities in Kongo initially saw no problem with the trade, since it was an extension of the institution of slavery that already existed in Africa. Dom Affonso, the newly-Christian Kongolese king, sent his son and other members of his family to study in Portugal, and he himself wrote quite acceptable Portuguese. His letters to successive Portuguese monarchs ask for missionaries, priests, as well as wine for communion and flour to bake the host for Mass. These, he wrote, were far more important than any other trade good.

Dom Affonso's letters show that his anguish grew as it became clear that Africa was receding from the top of Portugal's concerns, as the riches of India began to eclipse the potential of Africa. That would continue until after the turn of the seventeenth century, when Portugal began to run into competition for the India trade. Then, it began to

Site if the first slave market in Europe at Lagos on the southern
coast of Portugal.

think seriously about profiting from the unexplored and sparsely settled lands that they claimed in the New World.

The wholesale transformation of large parts of this vast territory required workers for plantation agriculture. Local Amerindians were pressed into labor, but there were not enough to fill the demand. The Europeans were to blame for that, even though they had made only fleeting visits to the New World in the 100 years after "discovery". That contact, however, was enough to introduce unfamiliar diseases throughout Native American populations so when the Europeans turned their attention to exploiting these vast lands, many indigenous populations were already decimated. Many Amerindians died in the tropical lowlands, where they were relocated to work on sugar cane and other plantations. Europeans turned to Africa for labor, because the populations there were more accustomed to hot, humid climates. In some cases, too, the Africans were prized because they were used to handling horses and cattle, with which Amerindians had no experience.

It is estimated that between 1450 and 1900, when slavery was outlawed throughout the Western Hemisphere, more than eleven million slaves were transported from Africa to the New World. Between 1650 and 1900, by far the largest number came from the former kingdoms of Kongo and Angola, an estimated forty percent of slaves sent to the Americas. In all, about four million slaves were sent to Brazil, 2.5 million to the Spanish Empire, two million to the British West Indies, 1.6 million to the French West Indies, a million to other European colonies and continental Europe, and half a million to British North America and the United States. It was without a doubt the largest transfer of human population until the mostly-voluntary trans-Atlantic European migrations beginning in the mid-nineteenth century. Even in North America where far fewer slaves were imported, they made up a large proportion of the population: by 1760, Africans and their descendants accounted for more than 20 percent of the population of the Thirteen Colonies. or 327,000. Since slavery was uneconomic in the northern colonies, this population was concentrated in the Carolinas, Virginia, Delaware, Maryland and Georgia, which meant in some regions Africans outnumbered Europeans.

The social fabric of the Kongo was fundamentally changed by the demand for slaves. When King Dom Affonso died, the issue of who was to succeed him led to violent internal conflict. This played into the hands of the Portuguese, since the war produced captives who could be sold as slaves. Other European countries would come to profit from similar conflicts elsewhere in Africa, although the papal authority behind Portugal's monopoly of trade with Africa was strong enough for Portuguese diplomats to persuade Edward IV of England to stop a planned expedition to Africa in the 1480.

Portuguese trade in Africa, as well as that in India and later Brazil, was dependent on two other kinds of coercion. One was the use of transportation to colonies as a penalty for crimes. Between 1670 and 1775 Portugal's population never exceeded two million, but it exiled about 50,000 criminals, the same number as did the British Isles, even though Britain's population was two to five times larger during the period. France, whose population was even larger—from 16 to 24 million—in all sent out only 51,000 free or forced colonizers to the New World. But not all Portuguese exiles were serious offenders; Portugal's bard Camões only escaped being imprisoned for irregularities in his customs accounts by agreeing to go to the Estado da Índia. Many of the Portuguese deportees prospered in their new countries.

Slaves were an integral part of life in Brazil until slavery ended in 1889.

The second kind of coercion has it roots in the the forced conversions of Jews and Muslims in continental Portugal. The Portuguese Inquisition focused much of its energy on looking for latent Judaism among New Christians. Many were crudely expelled; in 1493, 2,000 Jewish children of Spanish parents living in Portugal were packed up and sent to São Tomé. Others went more or less willingly: Garcia da Orta's decision to go to India has been attributed to his desire as a New Christian to escape discrimination in Portugal. The Brazilian merchant class of the eighteenth century was largely made up of New Christians, and many observers conclude that Portugal's loss in terms of talented, energetic citizens was the colony's gain.

The inland capital which was the seat of Dom Affonso, Kongo's convert king, was deemed inappropriate for the Portuguese headquarters as they widened their reach around the world. São Salvador/Mbanza Kongo was located days away from the Kongo or other navigable river. Furthermore, an inland kingdom, no matter how rich, was no match for a port when it came to controlling territory and trade, as the Portuguese success in the Indian Ocean and the Spice Islands at the edge of the Pacific Ocean proved.

As the slave trade grew, the need also grew for citadels and warehouses on the coast where slaves could be mustered for shipment across the Atlantic. Elmina and the islands of São Tomé and Principe off the coast just slightly south of the equator became major way stations for the Portuguese slave trade to the New World. But as more and more slaves were taken from Kongo and its neighbors, another slave trading port was needed farther south than São Tomé and Principe.

Luanda, now the capital of Angola, was begun in 1575 as São Paulo de Loanda with 100 families of Portuguese settlers and 400 Portuguese soldiers. Built on an island near the mouth of the Cuanza River, it was south of the immense and dense tropical forest that straddles the equator, but not so far south that its hinterland was desert. While still unhealthy for Europeans whose resistance to malaria and other tropical diseases was less than that of local populations—and it should be noted that one of the reasons why relatively few African settlements were on the coast was because native Africans also succumbed to disease—it offered perhaps the best anchorage on the west coat of Africa south of the equator. The cathedral and the houses of the elite were built on slightly higher land, which is what the Portuguese had grown accustomed to doing since their struggle to expel the Moors. The air was considered healthier there, and the height put the town above places where waste water might collect and contaminate drinking water supplies. The city became the administrative head of Portugal's African adventure in 1627. It continued to be Portugal's lynchpin in West Africa until the end of the colonial wars in 1974.

One of the most eloquent witnesses to what Luanda, and Angola, too, had become by then is the novelist Antonio Lobos Antunes. As a young doctor he was sent to do military service there in 1971. He wrote to his new wife in Lisbon almost daily. One letter was written "on this Sunday of unsupportable heat from a terrace looking out on the bay, while the fishing boats of the Blacks pass slowly from one shore to the other with tropical insolence, and big bizarre birds, cousins of seagulls, rise and fall without moving their wings above the palm trees in the gray and unmoving air." He goes on in another letter: "Only the soil is red ... and the nights are inhabited by the murmur of leaves and of insects drowning in a bathtub of sweat." And when he goes up-country, the trip takes nearly a week by bus, train and truck. "The misery of the locals is overwhelming. The villages are drowning in under-nourished skeletons, in contrast with the majesty of the landscape which is of a terrible beauty."

This is the legacy of 400 years of slave trading and colonialism, from which both Angola and Portugal are recovering. After the Portuguese pulled out, a bitter civil war tore the country apart for twenty-six years. (The other large Portuguese African colony, Mozambique, had a post-independence civil war that lasted sixteen years.) More recently the discovery of oil reserves off the coast of Angola has meant that a measure of prosperity has arrived. Currently Luanda is one of the most expensive cities in the world in which to rent or buy modern housing and offices, although its slums are as bad as any in Africa. Nevertheless the country boasts that it has the highest rate of economic growth in Africa. It proudly hosted the Africa Cup of Nations soccer competition in January 2010.

The last slave ship left Luanda 150 years ago, but the ancestors of Harvard professor Peter Gomes probably did not pass through the port on their way to New World servitude. On his mother's side Gomes appears to be descended from people who were enslaved farther north on the African continent. DNA testing done for the PBS television series shows he is related to Fulani, Tikar and Hausa peoples who lived in regions that now are in Nigeria and Cameroon, and this would suggest they were shipped from Elmina or Sierra Leone. It's through his father's family that Gomes is connected with the Portuguese, including that New Christian who probably left Portugal to avoid the Inquisition. On that side Gomes is descended from Africans who were transported to Cape Verde when the islands were being developed as a transshipment point for slaves.

Ribeira Grande was the name of the colony's capital. Founded in 1462, it was the first city built by Europeans in the tropics, and was, at one time, among the richest cities in the Portuguese empire. Vasco da Gama called in on his outward voyage to the Indies in 1498, and the following year Christopher Columbus stopped on his way back from his third trip to the New World. The city became the place where shipments of human cargo, brought in from various parts of Africa, were bought and sold. By the end of the sixteenth century, the city's wealth attracted not only Portuguese bent on making their fortune in the slave trade, but also pirates. The English adventurer Sir Francis Drake attacked with 1,000 men in 1585, while in 1712 the French pirate Jacques Cassard sacked and burned the city, taking away plunder estimated at three million pounds sterling in value. The colony's capital was moved to a more easily defendable location in the late eighteenth century. Following an earthquake which blocked Ribeira Grande's harbor a few decades later, the town declined into a shadow of its former glory.

Now called Cidade Velha to avoid confusion with a city on another of the Cape Verde islands, it was named a UNESCO World Heritage site in June 2009. It is still easy to see the plan of streets and houses laid out more than 450 years ago with steep dark rock hills rising behind. The two churches, the rows of houses, the straight streets and the fortress on a hill bear witness to a plan made in anticipation of prosperity.

In the middle of the town square there is still a marble pillar marking the spot where thousands of Africans were sold in lots. But while tourists stop here to take pictures and shake their heads in sadness, to the local people, the pillar, the Pelourinho, is just a part of their daily lives. On a fine afternoon, some will be sitting in the shade in the square, playing cards on benches, enjoying the view. They are proud of their Creole culture. Ribeira Grande was, as UNESCO says, "the cradle of the first fully fledged mixed-race Creole society ... (It) is an important initial link in an intangible heritage shared by Africa, the Americas and Europe." There is much to be proud of here, including the rainbow of skin colors you'll see in the faces in the square. They bear witness to heritages as mixed as that of Peter Gomes and of millions of Brazilians whose ancestors passed through here too.

CHAPTER FIVE

Sex

THE COASTAL REGION of the Brazilian state of Pernambuco is hot and luxuriant. When Gilberto Freyre was a boy at the beginning of the twentieth century (he was born in 1900), Recife, the capital city, had a population of about 100,000 and roots that went back nearly 400 years. It is located on the great shoulder of South America that projects into the Atlantic, recalling that millions and millions of years ago Africa and South America fit together before the tectonic plates which form the earth's crust began to split apart along the mid-Atlantic ridge. (The Azores were born from that rupture.)

The first Portuguese explorers didn't make landfall here first, but further south, where prevailing winds carried them west in the *volta do mar*, that counter-intuitive maneuver which allowed Portuguese ships to swing away from Africa in order to round the Cape of Good Hope. But within a few years, the possibilities for growing sugar cane in Pernambuco became clear, prompting settlements where the Beberibe River meets the Capibaribe River and flows into the sea. The region has been a significant factor in the construction of Brazilian identity.

The afternoon is still, the late summer heat bears down. Gilberto, whose mother has always professed a deep Catholic faith, is a student at a Colegio Galreath, a secondary school run by affiliates of the American Southern Baptist Church. His father, who is also an attorney and judge, teaches Latin there, is a respected and even pivotal figure in the school. There is no doubt that young Gilberto, with his wide grin and his shock of wavy dark hair, is one of the institution's stars. Not only does he tutor other students, he is preparing to give a lecture based on Herbert Spencer's philosophy and what it means for "the problem of education in Brazil." Not bad for someone at age fifteen.

Gilberto Freyre at fifteen. His massive social histories of Brazil celebrated
the country's long history of racial mixing and the Portuguese "genius"
for life in the tropics.

But he is a boy with a body as well as a brain, and in the languorous afternoons his thoughts turn to a lovely young maid about his own age, with warm brown skin, downcast eyes and a special way of smiling at him. Then, according to Freyre's journals, thought gives way to action and they meet in a series of furtive, heated encounters in the shadows of hot afternoons.

His parents intervene and she is sent off to work for an aunt, but nevertheless they find a way to continue their passion for nearly a year. He will remember the encounter all his life, and when he's seventy-five and a world figure, he'll publish his journals from the time, writing of his early love in graphic detail. See, he will say, that is how it was with me from the beginning. I am a true son of Brazil. I love the women of this country, in all their multi-colored beauty, as did my forefathers who sired a nation unique in the world, a Brazil that is a proud mixture of African, European and Amerindian.

However, before then he will pass several years discovering the world, meditating on his country and his roots before expounding theories that will define Brazil in the twentieth century and have repercussions far beyond.

Freyre's origins appear to have been mostly European—Portuguese, German, Dutch—with some admixture of Amerindian genes. His family had long been associated with sugar cane cultivation on plantations and qualified as one of the old patriarchal families that he believed were the backbone of Brazilian society. By the time he was born, the family's fortunes had declined, and his father, while able to provide, had to work for a living. Previous generations drew their fortunes from their land and the slaves who worked it.

Slavery was outlawed in Brazil in 1889, when Freyre's parents were adolescents. When he was growing up, the economy of Pernambuco remained agricultural, and social organization reflected the centuries of domination by the planter class. Freyre's mother, he frequently recalled, was a flower of this society, a woman of deep kindness and Roman Catholic devotion. His father, however, was part of the modern-izing force of the country. He was well educated, and sent his boys— Gilberto had a brother Ulisses—to the American-staffed school because it was considered about the best in the city; despite its Baptist affiliation many sons of Recife's Catholic elite were students there.

Gilberto was not a promising student at first; apparently he didn't learn to read until he was eight, much to the consternation of his parents. Yet perceptive teachers saw that he was a child of unusual intelligence and insatiable curiosity. Once he began to read, he did not stop, and by the time his secondary course was finished, his brilliance was apparent. Further studies abroad were indicated, but since Europe was still at war, an alternative closer to home had to be found. Baylor University in Waco, Texas, where many of the teachers at the Colégio Gilreath had trained, seemed the next best alternative. So in 1917, at the age of seventeen, Freyre went to the United States. It was the beginning of a journey of five years that saw him return to Brazil with his eyes opened, and his ideas changed.

The transition to English did not present problems, it seems, since English was used at Colégio Gilreath. What did bother him was the encouragement of his professors, who recognized his intelligence, to put aside Brazil and Portuguese and prepare for an academic career in the U.S. As well, he was shocked to discover that people of African descent were often badly treated in Texas. In his memoir he recounts how he smelled scorched flesh one day and was told it was a Black person being burned. "Never had I thought that such a thing would be possible now in the United States of America. But it is. And Negroes are lynched, murdered and burned. It's not an isolated incident, either."

He was disappointed by the quality of his fellow students, many of whom were training to be Baptist ministers and missionaries. To the chagrin of his mother, he had become a Protestant before he left for Texas, but his experience at Baylor led him to question that faith. He was disillusioned that so many young Baptists were preparing to go abroad to spread the faith and change the world, but didn't see that much was wrong in their home country, including great poverty and discrimination in Negro neighborhoods and towns.

It took him longer to come to terms with his own country's multiracial past. After receiving a B.A. from Baylor, he went onto work on a Master's degree at Columbia University in New York. Initially he seems to have been influenced by what was called at the time "scientific genetics," the idea that the so-called black, brown and yellow "races" were inferior to the white "race," and that racial mixing had a "mongrelizing" effect on populations. Just how this thinking had shaped his own perceptions can be seen in an anecdote he recounted several times in later years. While in New York he encountered a trio of sailors—all obviously of mixed race—from the Brazilian navy on leave in the Big Apple. His first reaction was that they looked like caricatures of humans, and he was profoundly ashamed of them and of his country. But working with anthropologist Frederick Boas on his thesis "Social life in Brazil in the Middle of the Nineteenth Century" he learned to study culture closely and to reject the idea that racial differences were inborn.

When he finished he wasn't in any hurry to return to Brazil, but spent the better part of the next two years traveling. During this time, his eyes were opened even wider as he visited France, Germany and Belgium, spent time in Oxford, and wrote dispatches for Brazilian newspapers from Spain and Portugal. He travelled with two friends, one a son of the American South and the other a German, through the states of the old American Confederacy.

He did not come "home" until the mid-1920s when, for the first time, he went to the Brazil's largest city, Rio de Janeiro. Then the national capital, it was bubbling over with a generation of young people looking for a definition for their country—and for a good time.

In his memoir, he recounts one evening that illustrates the ferment, as well as his growing appreciation of what would become considered typical Brazilian culture: samba. He says he "went out for bohemian fun" one evening with classical composers Heitor Villa-Lobos and Luciano Gallet, a future district attorney who was the grandson of a Brazilian president, and another soon-to-be famous intellectual, Sérgio Buarque de Holanda—all young men of bourgeois white families. They listened to guitar music and drank cachaça (cane brandy) with Pixinguinha, Patricio and Donga, three black or mixed-race sambistas who would soon be the toast of Paris. The only thing missing, Freyre reports, was "a few cabrochinas" or "wenches" of mixed African and European descent.

It was during this period that he worked on his ground-breaking study of Brazil's origins and social history, *The Masters and the Slaves.* As he read and wrote, he came to believe that Brazil's brand of slavery was less terrible than that found in the U.S. because it was based on a more humane understanding of the relation between slave and master. In addition, because Brazil was no exception to the pattern which saw

According to Gilberto Freyre, the children of Brazilian planters, like this one depicted in 1843, and their slaves, created Brazil's "racial democracy."

Portuguese men of all social ranks formed alliances with African and mixed race women in Brazil. This painting by Carlos Julião, from the 18th century shows a white noble giving a love letter to a mulatto woman.

very few women sent out from Portugal, the men fathered families with both Amerindian and African women, leading to an extremely large mixed-race population that Freyre held was particularly well adapted to the climate. He quotes from letters back to Portugal from early explorers on the loveliness and the sexual openness of Amerindian women. The descriptions bring to mind the idyllic scene that Camões gives to Vasco da Gama and his crew on the homeward voyage when the mariners encounter an enchanted isle, full of fruit and comely maidens.

Freyre asserts that the groundwork for this willingness to mate with women of different races had been prepared back home in Europe where legends of the dark-eyed enchantress were common and intermarriage with Moorish invaders had once been frequent. Although he doesn't discuss the experience of Portuguese adventurers in India or Africa,

Freyre concludes that the Portuguese had a "talent for miscegenation." In Brazil, he wrote, this racial mixing had led to a kind of unique, admirable "racial democracy" that set the stage for a vibrant culture. This belief in the positive benefits of racial mixing was 180 degrees removed from his earlier attitudes and from calls coming from a portion of the Brazilian intellectual community to "whiten" the country by encouraging immigration from Europe. It also was counter to the idea of the purity of the Aryan race which was soon to become the battle cry of Nazi Germany with which the Brazilian government was on friendlly terms. Freyre's work—he wrote four long volumes of Brazilian social history and countless magazine and newspaper articles and many of his lectures are in print—reflected the Brazil that people saw around them. The population of Brazil was generally darker in the northeast region where the first great wave of forced African migration had gone. Lighter, more European-appearing people lived in the southern areas where Italians and Portuguese had been encouraged to settle from the late 1800s because their labor in the coffee plantations was particularly prized. As Caetano Veloso, the noted dissident and musician, says of his youth in the northeastern state of Bahia, where nearly everyone was visibly of mixed race, "We considered ourselves to be peaceful, affectionate, clean. It was unimaginable that anyone born here would want to live in another country." Freyre argues that such admirable evidence of the virtues of miscegenation proved Brazil's originality and worth.

But what has been the real extent of racial mixing? Among the scientific advances of the turn of the twenty-first century is the mapping of human genome and the discovery that frequencies of certain genes vary from one population to another. Research has been underway in Brazil and on the Iberian peninsula for several years.

It turns out that the folklore about the desirability of the dark-eyed enchantress may have some basis in fact in Portugal and Spain. According to research published in 2008, it appears that nearly twenty percent of the population of the Iberian peninsula have ancestors who were Sephardic Jews, while more than ten percent of the population probably has ancestors from North Africa. The researchers were studying the genes transmitted through the male lines—those found on the Y chromosome that determines whether one is male or female—and suggest that more intermarriage went on than was previously thought.

Among the men who tested positive for genes found in Sephardic Jews and North Africans were some who had no idea that there were ever any Jews or Moors in their family line. Just when the mixing occurred is not clear, but it seems that it must date from the massive conversions of the fourteenth and fifteenth centuries, when Jews and Muslims were forced to convert.

This was not the only time that sex and the fruit of sexual relations became a factor in determining the politics and faith of the Portuguese and their empire, consciously or unconsciously. The story of Portuguese expansion is male-driven, but its lasting success is a story of women, says Professor José Curto of York University. He cites parish and legal records from Luanda that demonstrate the care and pride with which African women married to Portuguese men insisted on their connection to Portugal. They were the ones who ensured that the language took root so far away from Europe.

That's the upside of sexual politics.

The downside is the manner in which marriage was used by the Portuguese elite to consolidate their riches and power for short term gains, to the long term detriment of the nation. A series of dynastic marriages began at the high point of Portuguese exploration at the end of the sixteenth century. The end came two generations later with the grandiose illusions of the young king Sebastião, three of whose four grandmothers were sisters. The cult surrounding his death on the battlefield and the messianic hope that he might return, which flourished during the sixty years when Spain ruled Portugal, has clouded this part of the story. How to criticize a mystical hero? Centuries later he remains a part of the Portuguese myth, and to say that he probably was more than a little delusional (as was his mother who was confined for most of her life because of madness) attacks an important element of the Portuguese narrative.

Ironically it was the robust, illicit sex of an earlier generation that eventually saved the day for the Portuguese nation. When the Spanish kings who took over after the death of Sebastião were finally thrown off in 1640, the heirs of royal bastards ascended the Portuguese throne. They traced their lineage to the children fathered by João I before he married the English princess Philippa of Lancaster and begat the Infante

Henrique and his illustrious brothers of exploration days. The Avis-Bragança dynasty would continue for another hundred years, with a series of kings who were more than adequate to the job. The major sexual misstep they made was to marry off Caterina de Bragança to Charles II in 1661, sending with her as a dowry Bombay, Tangier and £1 million sterling, the largest bridal payment ever awarded for a royal marriage. Royal marriages, while they can have wide reaching effects, occur infrequently because, almost by definition, not many people are royal. Far more common are the alliances of ordinary people, and from the beginning of European and African settlement in Brazil these alliances were frequently multiracial. When the Portuguese arrived, a large Amerindian population lived everywhere from the tropical forests of Amazonia to the seacoasts and the central grasslands. Just how many there were is impossible to determine, but estimates of 2.5 million are common. Despite the vicissitudes of slavery and disease, some of the groups held out for a long time. As anthropologist David Cleary points out regarding the Botocudo nation, they were able to maintain their independence into the 1830s and controlled the coast and interior within a hundred miles of Rio to the north, rather as if "hostile Amerindians controlled Connecticut and blocked the overland route from New York to Boston." In 2006 the Brazilian agency charged with the census put the number of indigenous people at about half a million. Because of those early inter-racial liaisons, genetic studies suggest, the average Brazilian, no matter what race he or she identifies with, is likely to have ten percent of genes from indigenous ancestors.

Between 1550 and 1850, an estimated four million Africans were imported as slaves into Brazil. During the same period, about 500,000 Europeans settled there. Most of the Europeans were men, which meant that establishing a family usually involved marrying or at least procreating with women of other races. One of the great intellectual families of Brazil is descended from such a union. The Buarques de Holanda—Chico, the singer, composer and dissident; his father, Sérgio whose *Raízes do Brasil* appeared shortly after Freyre's first volume; Cristovam, senator and presidential candidate, and Heloise, a literary figure of considerable note, are among the recent notable members of the family—can trace their ancestry back to a slave woman who married the owner of a sugar plantation in 1795. She was illiterate, but saw that her children were well-educated. The family's surname comes from Arnau de Hollanda, who arrived in a caravel in 1535.

The Buarque de Holanda story suggests one way that slavery was different in Brazil than in the American South. Marriage between master and slave in the U.S. was usually illegal. But marrying your owner was not the only way to escape bondage in Brazil. Because of the way slavery was organized, it seems to have been easier for slaves to buy their freedom in Brazil than in the U.S. or the Caribbean. In Brazil's rich mining state of Minas Gerais, for example, slaves from the mining regions of Africa were in great demand. They were often allowed to keep part of what they found. In cities, following a pattern that existed in Africa, owners sometimes hired out their slaves, pocketing the lion's share of the wages, but allowing the slave to keep some of the proceeds. Slaves were also sometimes freed by their masters as a reward for good service. The result was that long before slavery was officially abolished a sizable portion of the population consisted of free men and women of African descent. In the 1820s it amounted to nearly thirty percent of the population. In some regions the percentage was much higher. For example, more than forty percent of the 390,000 people who lived in Freyre's home region of Pernambuco in the early 1800s were free or freed Africans or their descendants, while slaves accounted for another twenty to twenty-five percent of the population.

People of mixed race were called "pardo" and "mulatto," among other terms, each carrying its own level of politeness and information about what specific racial mixture was in question. Even when a mixed-race person's birth was considered legitimate—and in the officially Catholic society of the day, legitimacy was very important for inheritance and social standing—they might be scorned. Nevertheless, over the colonial period many reached levels of influence. Among them were Antonio Vieira, a Jesuit diplomat, statesman and master of Portuguese prose, the composer Lôbo de Mestiquita, considered by some to be the equal of European ecclesiastical composers of the period, and a number of lawyers and doctors trained in Portugal. It was not uncommon for mixed-race men of prosperous families to be sent for advanced studied at Coimbra in the late eighteenth and early nineteenth century, at a time when no mixed-race men from North America traveled across the Atlantic except as curiosities. American slaveholders, even the most progressive, provided nothing comparable for their mixed-race offspring.

In North America, it must be remembered, all mixed race people, no matter what their or their ancestors' status as slave or free, no matter how distant their African ancestors, were—and still are—considered Negro. Until 50 years ago, in the U.S. they could be legally discriminated against. By contrast, by the middle of the nineteenth century, when the slave trade was abolished but before slavery itself was legislated out of existence in Brazil, the upper ranks of Brazilian society included many people of mixed race. The country was an empire from 1820 to 1890, and during that time several "people of color" received titles of nobility. One of them, the Viscount of Jequitinhonha, was evidently dark enough to fail the discriminatory Jim Crow laws in the U.S which barred people of color from many public places. He was sent there on a diplomatic mission but was refused admission to a series of hotels in Washington, and returned to Brazil in "deep disgust and indignation."

But the example par excellence of the accomplishment of Brazilians of mixed race in the nineteenth century is the writer Joaquim Maria Machado de Assis (1839-1908). His story would fall in the classic North American poor-boy-makes-good category, except the fact that he was of mixed race would have disqualified him from the Horatio Alger sweepstakes. His father was a house painter who is usually described as "mulatto," and his mother, a Portuguese washerwoman. They worked for the widow of a senator who obviously thought well of them, since she acted as young Joaquim's godmother. But he was sickly, suffering from epilepsy which plagued him all his life. His schooling was erratic; he picked up Latin from the parish priest, French from a baker, other basics in the school for girls where his step-mother worked as a candle maker, and typography from a mixed-race bookseller and printer. There his literary talent and intelligence were recognized, and by the time he was twenty-five his poetry had been published to much acclaim. It wasn't until he had passed through a long period of illness in mid-life that he began writing fiction, however, producing a body of work which some consider some of the best fiction of the late nineteenth century in any language.

Acceptance of mixed-race people did not eliminate either poverty among non-whites in Brazil nor the fear that large numbers of non-whites would have deleterious effects on the country. As pressure mounted for an end to slavery in the 1880s, owners of coffee plantations in particular began to look for workers in Europe. They were recruited in Italy, Portugal, Spain and Germany, but unlike immigration to North America, which steamship companies, railroad lines and even European governments had a vested interest in encouraging and frequently subsidized, these workers had to pay their passage. They found themselves with little chance to acquire land of their own once they arrived in Brazil. This wave of immigration was considerable, amounting to about 5.5 million people between 1872 and 1975. In addition to immigrants from Europe, beginning in 1908 more than half a million Japanese were recruited as agricultural workers. Today São Paulo has the largest Japanese community in the world outside of Japan.

These newcomers were expected to marry mixed-race Brazilians. Freyre roundly criticized Germans who settled in the south of the country because they didn't intermarry, and therefore didn't contribute to Brazil's "racial democracy." Underlying it all was the idea that miscegenation—outlawed in many of the states of the U.S. until it was ruled unconstitutional in a 1967 Supreme Court decision—was both desirable and to be encouraged.

When Brazilians were asked in 1872 to say what group they belonged to, nearly equal numbers self-identified as white or mixed-race "pardos" (in round numbers, 3.8 million compared to 3.7 million). Another two million considered themselves "black." (In the United States and Canada, blacks and pardos would have been lumped together as one group, so that the whites would be outnumbered.) Slightly more than 125 years later more than half of the 169 million Brazilians counted in the 2000 census (53.4 percent) said they were white, 6.1 percent said they were black and 38.9 percent, brown, with the rest self-declaring as Amerindian, Asiatic or other.

But color and race in Brazil are more complicated than what meets the eye or what group a person might consider him- or herself a part of. After four centuries of racial mixing the genetic heritage of Brazilians can only be guessed from an individual's appearance. In part that is because the genes for dark skin are not necessarily related to other characteristics and have been selected for around the world because dark skin provides some protection from the ravages of the sun: many of the people Vasco da Gama encountered on the West coast of India had skin as black as any found in Africa. Lighter skin, which makes it easier to produce Vitamin D in latitudes where days are short for part of the year, has evolved at least twice: Europeans and Northern Asians actually owe their light skin to different genetic mutations..

Today genetic studies indicate that Brazilians who call themselves "white" are likely to have up to forty percent of their genes associated with African descent. Furthermore, no matter what "color" men said they were in a study of a group of 200 unrelated males from four regions of Brazil, the vast majority had Y chromosomes containing markers of European origin, while only two percent had a Y chromosome lineage that came from Sub–Saharan Africa, and one percent that was of Amerindian origin. The study of genetic material that always comes through the maternal line showed far more equal distribution: European lineages accounted for thirty-nine percent, thirty-three percent were Amerindian and twenty-eight percent were African.

This is consistent with what we know about the peopling of Brazil. First there were the Amerindians, then came the Portuguese, nearly all male, who had children with Amerindian women, and later with African women, but who usually took a white wife when they could. The last hundred years has seen an influx of more European stock, which, after the first generation, has been absorbed into the great Brazilian mixture of which Freyre was so proud.

The result is that in the same family brothers and sisters may run the gamut in terms of skin tone, hair texture, and shape of nose and lips. They may even tell census takers that they belong to different racial groups.

It is a triumph for Freyre—or is it?

Mention his name in some circles today, and you get raised eyebrows. His ideas about racial mixing provided a powerful narrative for a couple of generations of people who wanted to see a world of racial equality and peace. But along the way Freyre either was co-opted or chose to become a spokesman for a conservative, fascist vision.

When Freyre's work was first published, Brazil had embarked on what would be nearly three decades of dictatorship. General Getúlio Vargas took office in 1930 with a populist program and a plan to unite the country, which had been torn by regional rivalries. Freyre's ideas about the Portuguese genius for racial mixing and his faith in the grand destiny of what he would later call "Lusotropicalism," were exactly what Vargas and his advisors needed. Using the new media of radio and film and emphasizing things like soccer and pride in the Brazilian "racial democracy," Vargas forged a united nation. It was called the Estado Novo, in an explicit reference to Portugal's Estado Novo, begun in 1926 with the first government of António Salazar.

Both men were inspired by the way Mussolini drew on the myths of Italy's past glory to unite it. Their admiration for Hitler was also apparent, but tempered by the usefulness they found in embracing multiracialism. At a time when Hitler was banning jazz as "Negro music," the Brazilian government saw no problem with including a largely black samba school band in a direct broadcast to Germany. Musicologist Hermano Vianna notes, "One would like to have seen the faces of the ideologues of Aryan supremacy (who, at the time, still hoped to establish a special relationship with the Brazilian government) as those Afro-Brazilian drums came pounding over the airwaves."

But Freyre's idea of Lusotropicalism and the supposed special ability of the Portuguese to adapt to tropical areas was just what Salazar needed to justify aggressive efforts to increase the Portugal's presence in its African colonies. Freyre apparently didn't object to this, and allowed himself to be honored by both the Portuguese and Brazilian Estado Novo governments. When a second dictatorship took control of Brazil in the 1960s after a short democratic period, Freyre did not speak out against repressive measures aimed at silencing dissidents. In so doing he cut his links with many of the elements in Brazilian society that had found his work so edifying.

Brazil never was a true "racial democracy," Freyre's critics argued. Brazilian society might have many mixed race people as the result of centuries of sex—and frequently love—between people with varied ancestries, but the darker one is, the poorer one is likely to be. Freye's critics said that his classifications were simplistic, and that he did not understand (or chose not to understand) the role that racial discrimination has played in Brazilian society from colonial times. In fact when democracy returned in the late 1980s Brazil had the second highest level of income distribution inequality in the world, after Sierra Leone. Freyre, who died in 1987, was cited less and less, and for more than a decade he was rarely mentioned with approval in the higher circles of

Brazilian intellectual and cultural life.

But everything that goes around comes around. At the turn of the twenty-first century when Brazilian politics took a turn to the left, Freyre was to some extent rehabilitated. Ironically, his reputation was in part salvaged by another son of Pernambuco, Luís Inacio Lula da Silva, whose background was practically the inverse of Freyre's.

Born in a town in the interior, the seventh of eight children, Lula moved with his family south to São Paulo state as a young boy, following the promise of better economic conditions. He started work at twelve, trained as a lathe operator, and then worked in the metal industry where he became involved in union activities, which led to the organization of the Parti Trabalhadores, the PT or Workers' Party. He ran for president of the country in 1989, 1994 and 1998, and was finally elected in 2002 with a significant majority.

Part of this victory was due to an alliance with other, center-left parties, but a good deal of the credit is due to the energy of the man, who in many ways embodies the hopes of perhaps the majority of Brazilians. And, significantly, he launched his first winning presidential campaign at the Porto Alegre conference on world poverty by reciting an elegy to Brazil written by Freyre in 1926 which celebrates the multitudinous variety of the nation. It begins "I hear the voices, I see the colors, I see the races, I sense the footsteps of that other Brazil which is coming, more tropical, more brotherly, more Brazilian."

The recitation—full of emotion and hope and delivered in Lula's charismatic style—brought down the house. It seemed to be what Brazilians wanted to hear and believe about themselves. It should be no surprise that the verse has been made into a video aimed at boosting national pride and to celebrate Freyre.

Another video, this one from 2010, was made in Recife, during Brazil's version of Carnaval. It is hot, because February is late summer in the Southern Hemisphere and because of the beat of the samba schools, the dancing flesh, the heightened awareness of the beauty of the young bodies moving in time to rhythms that shake the senses. The dancers touch bellies, suggesting other touches that might follow once the dance is over. As sociologist Richard G. Parker says, "Rising up from the feet and filling the entire body with life, the movement of the (dance) opens out like the outstretched arms that are among the most characteristic gestures of the carnaval to ... embrace the world." The dance "frees the body from the daily constraints imposed upon it, defying sadness and suffering. ... Like the symbolism of carnaval more generally, it celebrates the flesh. It focuses on the sensuality of the body. It offers a vision of the world given over to pleasure and passion, joy and ecstasy." The words being sung are in Portuguese with the particular accent of Brazil. They are a tribute to a nation whose genius was founded as much in its loins as elsewhere. When the question is asked, how did the Portuguese build and keep their empire with so few boots on the ground, part of the answer surely is, because the boots frequently were taken off—along with everything else.

Machado do Assis, considered the best writer working in Portuguese in the nineteenth century, was of mixed race parentage.

CHAPTER SIX

Cities and Strong Men

VIDEOS LIKE THE ONES of Carnaval revelers in Recife provide quick, easily accessible glimpses of what people are feeling and thinking today. The same kind of candid picture for other historical periods is much rarer. There is no dearth of courtly life in paintings or tapestry, but you won't find much about the life of ordinary people. The Portuguese, however, have a treasure trove of images dating back to the fifteenth century that often present a vision of many levels of society. One panoramic view of Lisbon in the early 1700s, in particular, says a lot about the delicate balance that exists between history made by *o povo*, the people, and history as it is forged by great men and leaders. In comparing the two visions, it is possible to appreciate another aspect of the Portuguese adventure—leadership over the centuries. What happened in the Lisbon of the eighteenth century is worth contrasting with the invention of Brasília three hundred years later.

The panorama is merely one of the largest of a wealth of *azulejos,* those images in small squares of painted and fired tile that you find everywhere in Portugal and everywhere the Portuguese traveled.. The term comes from Arabic *azzelij* (or *al zuleycha, al zuléija, al zulaiju, al zulaco*), meaning a small piece of polished stone, which originally referred to the stone mosaics that reached perhaps their greatest beauty in Byzantine times. But because the word is similar to the Portuguese word for blue, *azul,* and because many of the loveliest azulejos are blue, it's sometimes wrongly thought that there is some relation to the Persian word for the lovely blue semi-precious stone lapis lazuli. Not so, although the confusion is another reflection of the way ideas and goods have traveled widely over the centuries.

But let's take a close look at the Lisbon panorama. It now is on display in a Lisbon museum dedicated to azulejos, a treasure house

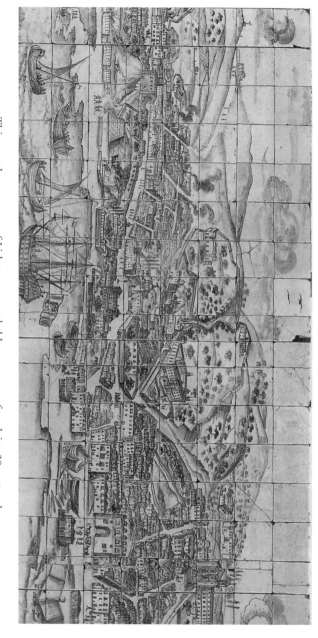

This grand panorama of Lisbon, a remarkable sequence of azulejos 30 metres long, was completed in 1743, twelve years before the earthquake that devastated the city. (Detail seen here.)

devoted to the art form. The foreground of the nearly thirty-meter-long (thirty-three feet) long creation shows the waterfront of Lisbon with the mighty River Tagus rolling along, fishing boats leaving the shore, sailors rowing in from caravels. Men are standing and talking near a place where it looks like a boat could tie up. To the right, what looks like a funeral procession passes, carrying a coffin. Two riders on horseback cross a great open space that could be a parade ground. They appear to be heading towards a group of buildings which are higher than the three low warehouses right next to the water. Four blocks of two- and three-story buildings are behind, in front of another open space. Just beyond rises a still more substantial group of structures, surrounded by a wall which also encloses a bell tower. In the distance hills covered with groomed trees indicate the limits of the city. The scene is calm, a morning at a time when it appeared that Portugal would rule the world. The bells in the many churches can almost be heard. The wind that fills the sails of the ships on the river practically ruffles your hair.

The art of the azulejos had been flourishing for centuries in Spain. Moorish artisans had long decorated mosques and residences with beautiful, frequently geometric designs. Dom Manoel, the Portuguese king at the end of the fifteenth century, brought back a passion for the tiles when he visited Spain in 1498, the year of Vasco da Gama's voyage to India. As treasure flowed into Portuguese coffers, some of the riches were used to pay for decorations for the Mosteiro dos Jerónimos near the Praia das Lágrimas and to build churches and cover their walls and those of public buildings and noble residences with tiles. The popularity of azulejos has continued ever since.

The grand panorama of Lisbon was finished in 1743 and it provides a graphic record of the city just twelve years before the violent earthquake and tsunami destroyed it and shook the foundations of belief throughout Europe. It portrays houses perched on the edge of Lisbon's hills with an insouciance that seems foolhardy, particularly given the fact that large earthquakes had shaken the city frequently: the one in 1555 left 2,000 dead.

But disasters of this sort were not high in the consciousness of Lisbon's ordinary folk, let alone that of the upper classes, many of whom spent much time in hedonistic enjoyment. Convents, for example, were reputed to be places where many ladies of noble birth secluded themselves, not to follow a religious life but to carry on amorous adventures.

The young king who took the throne in 1750 was a simple man who may have suffered from the fact that he was the offspring of a couple who shared Phillip William, Elector of Palatine, as a grandfather; Portuguese royalty all too often succumbed to the temptation of intermarrying in order to keep control of titles and land within a family. The monarch was very happy to turn over effective control of his country to an ambitious and extremely competent diplomat and administrator, Sebastião José de Carvalho e Melo, later made Marquês de Pombal. When the Great Earthquake struck on the morning of November 1, 1755, the king and his family were actually at their country estate at nearby Ajuda. They had left the city after early Mass because one of the children had persuaded the family to pass the All Saint's holiday in the bucolic grounds on the hills west of Lisbon.

Thousands of more modest people were not so lucky. The earthquake appears to have been caused by a slippage of tectonic plates off Portugal's east coast, and to have measured something like nine on the Richter scale of intensity. (In comparison, the Chilean quake of February 2010 measured 8.8 while the Haitian one a month earlier was 7.2.) The quake was felt as far away as Finland and the north coast of Africa, with damage concentrated in Portugal, southwestern Spain and Morocco. In Lisbon distinct shocks were felt over a ten-minute interval, causing immediate damage to many buildings, including the cathedral where mid-morning services had just finished. But worse followed when a tsunami triggered by the seismic movement raced toward the shore, and into the mouth of the Tagus. Waves three meters (ten feet) high swept in and then out again, destroying buildings, ships and quays. A massive fire followed that burned for at least five days.

The quake prompted considerable discussion and philosophic musings throughout Europe, particularly since it occurred on one of the major feast days of the Roman Catholic religious calendar, and because many innocent souls were killed as they worshipped. In a celebrated poem about the disaster written the following year, Voltaire questioned the doctrine that everything is for the best in this best of all possible worlds. "Without doubt everything is arranged, everything is ordained by Providence," he wrote in his preface, "but it seems equally true that for a very long time everything hasn't been arranged for our welfare."

In the face of such destruction, the king mandated Pombal to rebuild the fallen city. He had the right man for the job, it would appear.

In the many appreciations of Pombal which have been written in the 250 years since he was removed from power after the death of the king he served, he has frequently been called in an enlightened despot, a philosopher king in everything but royal title. Pombal had extensive diplomatic experience in Vienna and London. He had a wide circle of friends who included some of the best thinkers of the age as well as Portuguese expatriates who had been forced to leave the country due to the Inquisition. When he was tapped by the king to take over administration of the country, he had a kit bag of ideas about governmental organization, economic policies and education. He had reflected considerably on the old conundrum of how to protect national interest challenged by enemies who are ready to fight over territory (think France or Spain) while somehow keeping in check maritime allies who are also commercial rivals (think England). "Support rarely came cost-free," historian Kenneth Maxwell comments in his biography of Pombal.

Maxwell goes on, "This period, especially after the 1750s, is seen in Portugal as being the very embodiment of the Enlightenment." It brought the first system of state-supported education, complete reform of the University of Coimbra (which had been one of the first universities in Europe), reduction of the Inquisition's powers, modernization of the army, double entry bookkeeping, fiscal reforms and a serious attempt to improve agriculture including the establishment of the first system for regulating the provenance of wines. It did not go unnoticed that one of the first approved *apelação* was a vineyard in the Douro region owned by Pombal himself. "It was a regime inspired by an absolutism of reason, and its authoritarianism was essential to the process of reestablishing national control over the economy and revitalizing the state" which had been begun to stagnate.

To much of the old aristocracy, Maxwell adds, Pombal was an upstart, a near-nobody where blood and lineage were concerned. Furthermore, like some among the younger nobility who saw what was happening in prosperous England and Holland, Pombal was convinced that despite the riches from Brazil, Portugal was losing ground because families engaged in trade were not ennobled and because so many Jews and New Christians had been chased from the country during the ravages of the Inquisition.

Among his decrees were the end of discrimination against New Christians, and the replacement of the Inquisition with a sort of police force. He also undertook what Maxwell calls a frontal attack on the racial prejudices of the Portuguese clergy in Goa. "His Majesty regards everyone as equally noble and qualified for all posts and offices, whether military, political and civil ... besides all whites and browns, being equally vassals of His Majesty it is no way in conformity with Divine Law, Natural Law and the Law of Nations that foreigners be permitted to exclude natives from cultivating the land of their birth, or from the offices and benefits there of," Pombal declared.

He insisted on good reporting of what was going on in the colonies. Local authorities in all of them were supposed to send in detailed accounts which included censuses of the populations at a time when a thorough census had yet to be undertaken in Portugal itself; we have a more definite idea of the population of Luanda in the 1760s than we do of Lisbon.

It was a man of rare talent, energy and intelligence who took on the task of rebuilding Lisbon. It appears that the city had a population of about 300,000 at the time of the earthquake, including a good 10,000 who were of African descent. It had grown down from the hill fortified by the Moors to fill the low land between it and hills to the west. A new palace and opera house had recently been built, while a half dozen handsome churches completed the scene. But by the time fires had burned themselves out after the earthquake, the waterfront and much of the sumptuous new construction was gone. So were churches like the gothic Carmo, which now stood like a ghostly skeletons of their former beauty.

Pombal acted swiftly. Looters were summarily hanged while rents and prices for food and building material were frozen at pre-earthquake levels. The dreadful problem of what to do with the decaying bodies of earthquake victims was solved by getting permission from Church authorities to take the corpses out to sea, where they were weighed down and tossed overboard. Then Pombal turned to men with technical training to plan the rebuilding, refusing to grant any permits until the masses of rubble had been cleared and the plan for rebuilding established.

The low land, which was the center of Lisbon, was wiped out in the great
earthquake of 1755. Under the directon of the Marquês de Pombal the center
of the city was rebuilt on rational lines inspired by the Enlightenment.
In the distance is the Castelo São Jorge, a remnant of former days.

The Marquês de Pombal was authoritarian but his work included doing away with the Inquisition and slavery in Portugal itself, as well as making Lisbon a model city.

The earthquake, however dreadful it might have been, was an opportunity for change that Pombal was not going to allow to escape his Enlightened wisdom. After the Great Fire of London in 1666, a portion of the center of that city was rebuilt along lines suggested by Christopher Wren. In the early 1700s, Turin had been expanded beyond the city walls, following plans which featured squares and streets laid on grids. Pombal and his head planner looked to these major changes in urban structure for ideas, but in the end forged ahead to plan a new city center that was the largest urban reconstruction project ever undertaken until Napoleon III hired Baron Georges-Eugène Haussmann to remake Paris more than a hundred years later.

Several things are remarkable about the project. One was the way that pre-cut wooden shelters, called *barrocos*, were built from wood purchased in North Sea countries, in order to provide temporary shelters for the people of the ravaged city. Some of the shelters were rudimentary, but others were elaborate. The king and his family lived in one for several years; the monarch was so traumatized by the experience of the earthquake that he did not want to go inside stone buildings for a long time.

The reconstruction plan also exhibited remarkable concern for hygiene. Some of the buildings in Lisbon had been connected to sewers, and if the land use patterns were to be changed, the sewer connections would have to be modified too. One solution would be to allow waste to run down the middle of the streets as was done in many other cities. Another would be to have night soil carts collect waste on a regular basis. Both of these would mean that buildings would have to have glazed windows to keep out the inevitable stench, the chief engineers noted.

The most expensive, but surely more desirable, was to connect newly built houses to sewer pipes buried under the street so that the waste would run unseen and unsmelled to the river. This was the solution adopted, and if complete sewage treatment arrived only in the early twenty-first century, Lisbon enjoyed an underground system of sewage collector pipes at a time when London was ferrying night soil up the Thames to be dumped in fields and Napoleon's reworking of Paris's sewer system was fifty years in the future.

Making that decision did not solve the problem of exactly how to lay out the rebuilt city, however. Some thought was given to moving the most important buildings and the port facilities about ten kilometers west to Belém. Structures there had suffered relatively little damage. The chapel at the Mosteiro had a few cracks, but the tsunami did not jump the sand banks which stood off the shore. But such a move was rejected. The adopted plan was to lay out the streets on the devastated low land, the Baixa, rationally, along a grid with buildings of a height that would be safe in a future quake and where sunlight would reach the ground level for most of the year. The plan echoed the street grid of the Bairro Alto which had been laid out when that land was opened for development a century earlier. Such a large scale reworking on lines which reflected Enlightenment rationality was unique in Europe. It was to inspire at least two other town plans in the Portuguese empire, in Brazil and in Goa, but has passed unremarked and unappreciated in European capitals.

The Portuguese historian and urbanist José-Augusto França says this is because Portugal had its back to Europe, and did not inspire a particular school of architecture or town planning. "Nowhere but in the Baixa does one find an urban ensemble which uses as its axis two grand but functional open spaces," he writes. The grand squares called the Rossio and the Praça do Commercio still anchor the center of the city today.

Also innovative was the way that standardized elements were mandated for the reconstruction—window and door shapes of fixed dimensions, as well as interlocking designs for the azulejo trim, for example—in order to profit from economies of scale in their fabrication. And eighty years before the "invention" of the balloon frame style of building in the United States which dramatically lowered construction costs and increased ease and rapidity of building, Pombal's crews came up with the *gaiola* or cage style of wood framing. The impetus was the observation that wood was more resilient than stone during earthquakes. The principle is the same as that used in the strong, light wood-framed house developed in the 1830s in Chicago, and which is used in modified form today. But, while the boards in Lisbon were cut to standard sizes, they were attached with mortise and tenon joints, not nails. Milled boards and mass-produced nails would have to wait until the Industrial Revolution had really begun to roll.

By then Pombal would be long gone—replaced soon after the king died—and winds of change would have blown through Europe. Revolution

Gaiola, which means "cage" in Portuguese was the basis of the rebuilding of Lisbon. Using pre-cut, standardized lumber, the earthquake-resistant contruction had no equivalent until the invention of "balloon frame" construction 80 years later in the United States.

rocked France, followed by the rise of Napoleon. There were more dynastic battles within the Portuguese royal family. The entire Portuguese court spent nearly twenty years in Brazil, where it took refuge following the advance of Napoleon on the Iberian Peninsula. Brazil declared itself an independent empire, with a ruler from the Portuguese royal family.

One of the first things that was proposed for Brazil was a new capital. As a Portuguese colony, the seat of government had been Rio de Janeiro since 1763, but it was thought that the port city presented security risks. Building a new capital would divorce governance from regional rivalries in the vast country, as well as being a statement about the future of the new nation which was already more populous than Portugal. New capitals are common desires of new countries. Washington, D.C., itself a massive planned community that only reached it potential 150 years after its founding, was a compromise between Southern interests and the rival colonial cities of Philadelphia, New York and Boston. Both Canada and Australia opted for new cities as part of their nation-building effort; the places which became Ottawa and Canberra were nothing more than sleepy settlements before their election as capitals over the heads of their larger, more influential rivals.

But it was not until the middle of the twentieth century, 125 years after the first proposal, that Brazil plunged headlong into a project to build a new capital in the interior. The country was in the midst of a short democratic period between dictatorships when Juscelino Kubitschek promised in 1955 that, were he elected president, he would see a new city called Brasília built by the end of his five year term. It was an audacious proposal, and probably bigger in relative terms than rebuilding Lisbon two centuries earlier.

Brazil had had some experience in producing master plans for new cities. At the turn of the twentieth century Belo Horizonte, the capital city of the state of Minas Gerais, of which Kubitschek had been governor, was laid out along classical Haussmannian city planning lines. It was built in five years. Brasília was planned from the beginning to be larger than Belo Horizonte, and to focus the world's eyes on Brazil. An international competition for a plan for the new city was opened shortly after Kubitschek was elected president of the country. The architect for the major buildings had been chosen—Oscar Niemeyer—who already had a distinguished career, including the design of the United Nations headquarters in New York. Teams of urban planners submitted proposals for the overall plan, most with pages and pages of descriptions as well as drawings and technical details. But five out of six jurors voted for a schematic but visionary design that fit on four large cards, with nary a technical drawing nor plan attached.

The winner of the urban planning competition, Lúcio Costa, took the relatively flat land of Brazil's central plain and proposed a spread-out city that would be monumental. Frequently, its layout is compared to a bird with outstretched wings or an airplane seen from above. The central axis would feature broad, automobile-friendly thoroughfares along which the buildings of government would be set, housing executive, legislative and judicial arms of the government as well as all the ministries. Extending out from either side would be curving boulevards of housing, the north and south wings, the *Asa sul* and *Asa Norte*. Organized in super blocks which would have a population large enough to support an elementary school and neighborhood services, the basic style was a six- or seven-story apartment building with elevators, along with three-story walk-up buildings and a few ranks of row housing.

At the time cities around the world were building big housing projects: Singapore had begun its plan to re-house its entire population in flats, France was building high-rise blocks in Parisian suburbs and flirting with apartment towers in central Paris, Robert Moses had plans to pave over New York's Greenwich Village, and nearly every U.S. city was tearing down inner city neighborhoods to "renew" them by re-housing their residents in high-rise public housing. Only Singapore took seriously the puzzle of integrating work and housing and linking the two with good public transportation. The rest were failures, for the most part, and in egregious cases, resulted in North American cities like Chicago and St. Louis tearing down the new housing after a few decades because they simply did not work.

Brasília was, of course, a much bigger endeavor than modifying portions of an existing city. Kubitschek was also the driving force behind the development of a Brazilian automobile industry, so one of the tenets of the plan was that the private vehicle would be king. The new city was intended to be the place where Brazilian technical ability and esthetic skill would be uniquely combined in a setting that would capture the imagination of the rest of the world.

And because Brasilia's planners wanted to make sure that the grand outline of the new capital would be clear from the beginning, the city did not grow out from a central core. Distances between government buildings were designed to be large so that the structures would stand out against the emptiness of the public spaces. Construction went on in all parts of the basic plan from the beginning. The result was a raw new city where distances were usually too far to walk, and where the major non-private means of transportation—buses and passenger-carrying trucks—were frequently too expensive for the workers to use to commute to work.

Little thought seems to have been given to where to house the thousands and thousands of construction workers who flooded into the new city to find work. Part of the argument for relocating the capital to the interior of the country was to encourage development in the even more sparsely settled regions farther to the west. Planning to house the new work force adequately might have made Brasília a jumping-off point from which workers and their families could move on once the new city was built. Costa said several times that he intended his housing to be socially and economically integrated, that all levels of income would be able to live together. But this was a goal more honored in the breach than in the attainment.

And initially there was practically no place to live in at all. One work camp was opened within weeks of the announcement of the project, but it was far too small. Makeshift shelters sprang up at once, with no planning, no sewage, no water, and no transportation. In the end the government had to try to integrate these informally built neighborhoods into a larger plan for the metropolitan area. They also had to think about public transportation because after initial construction was over thousands of workers continued to live in the makeshift developments since they could not afford housing in the elegant new city.

Kubitschek was democratically elected, but that his style of governance had its roots in the long period of the Vargas dictatorship, the Brazilian Estado Novo from 1930 to 1954. Begun to provide stability after fifty years when power shifted back and forth between the centers

Oscar Neimeyer designed most of Brasília's buildings, including the National Congress bulding.

of São Paulo and Minas Gerais, the Vargas regime was overtly populist in its social programs but fascist when it came to human rights. Decisions were made at the top—with the best intentions in the world, or so the public was told—and the results descended to the other layers of society. It is incorrect to talk of a "trickle down" effect, because the impact on lower social classes was frequently far more direct and devastating than the gentle rain that "trickle" suggests.

Modernist ideas of city design and architecture in the early and mid-twentieth century went hand in hand with this. They denied the possibility that the past had value and, smitten with technological wonders like cars, elevators and concrete, tried to create city-machines that were "safely zoned and physically healthy to function perfectly," as one urban planner puts it. Old patterns, many of them the result of slow adaptation to circumstances, necessity and geography, were swept away.

Take the grid pattern for streets, for example. The usual pattern for the growth of urban settlement since men and women began to live in groupings larger than an extended family was determined by topography and land use. The Romans built straight roads, to be sure, but until the seventeenth century they were the exception. The oldest sections of Lisbon are good examples of this kind of organic land pattern: the old Alfama district is a near-labyrinth of narrow streets twisting and turning up and down the hill, perhaps avoiding a big tree which grew in one place several hundred years ago, but of which there exists no trace today. Beginning in the sixteenth century though, more consideration was frequently given to laying out new streets. In Lisbon itself, the opening of the hillside district west of Alfama produced a more regular pattern of streets in the Bairro Alto, while later additions to the city were frequently laid on a grid. Then came Pombal's plan for the area destroyed in the Great Earthquake.

In the Spanish Empire the desire for regularity and order led to the choice of town sites on broad places where a grid could be easily developed. But in the territories touched by the Portuguese, other considerations were given weight. For example, a site frequently was chosen because it was easily defended, following a pattern dear to the Portuguese ever since they fought their way south against the Moors in the eleventh century. Vila do Porto on the island of Santa Maria, the original settlement at Luanda, Angola, and Olinda, the first settlement at Recife,

Brazil, are good examples of building on high ground with good views of the harbor. These settlements, as well as Pombal's plan for Lisbon, were predicated on people and goods getting around on foot; the grids were on a human scale, and when monuments or plazas were included, they were only large enough to impress a single standing person, not to overwhelm him or her.

Brasília, however, was conceived on a completely different scale. It has no commanding hills. The site was chosen in part because of its gentle, sloping terrain that promised good drainage as well as ease of construction. The relative flatness meant that there could be unimpeded views of the monumental buildings Niemeyer would design. The topographic features which make the city interesting—the wrap-around lake and the slightly graded rise toward the monuments—are the products of massive earth moving.

Fifty years later, the original plan, the Plano Pilato, classed a UNESCO World Heritage site, is still visible although the Brasília metropolitan area is considerably different from what Costa and Niemeyer envisaged. From the air and on maps the curves of the two residential "wings" can clearly be seen, while the esplanade is filled—too filled, some say—with grand constructions that are intended to be both monuments to the genius of Brazil and to continue the city's heritage of groundbreaking architecture and urbanism. The city also is home to about 250,000 people, just as its planners foresaw. Surrounded by a greenbelt, which includes national parks and ecological reserves, it could be viewed as the fulfillment of a generation's dreams, as well as a tribute to what a few men with vision, and considerable power can accomplish.

However, the original city is a relatively small part of the metropolitan region. While some seventy percent of jobs are in the Plano Pilato area, only ten percent of the Federal District's 2.5 million population lives there. The Brasília of Kubetschek's plan is surrounded by sixteen suburban towns beyond the greenbelt. Some are reworkings of the squatters' settlements that went up during the 1960s. Others are more planned affairs, designed to relieve pressure on the central city. Those farthest away are reminiscent of those first rough and tumble shantytowns, usually built by the people who live in them with the same mixture of pride and desperation found in the favelas which surround other Brazilian cities. The satellite towns are linked to the Plano Pilato area by highways, and overall density is low, even though individual neighborhoods can be extremely dense. While a subway system leading out of the Plano Pilato was inaugurated in 2000 and is currently being expanded and the bus system is well developed (one of the first of the grand constructions was a bus terminal), the private automobile is what Brasilienses (one of the names for the residents of Brasília) aspire to. The result is a city which is a bad example in many ways of what a twenty-first century city should be. It has low carbon and energy efficiency levels since, even though it has many green and open spaces, walking or cycling are difficult because of the fragmentation of connecting roads and paths and the distances involved. Compared to Curitiba, another city in the interior of Brazil which has received considerable input from urban planners but of a different frame of mind, many say Brasília is a monument to a number of bad ideas.

What does this say about the role of leadership in governing a country? About the desirability of the Philosopher King?

To assess the contribution of visionary leadership, let us jump back in time to the grand panorama of Lisbon which is such a valuable record of what the city and Portugal was like before the Marquês de Pombal. The year that it was completed, 1743, thousands of slaves passed through ports controlled by the Portuguese, headed for the markets of the Western Hemisphere. France and England had been engaged in continuous rivalry, and frequent open war, for a hundred years. Glimmers of intellectual light shone in several European cities, as men (and sometimes women) struggled to consider how the world might be better ordered than it was. By the end of the century, thirteen of Britain's sixteen North American colonies had won their independence and embarked on a democratic experience that would be repeated all over the world. The French had deposed their monarch and declared in favor of the rights of man. And the institution of slavery was abolished in Portugal, making it the first European nation to do so.

Pombal gets the credit for that. To be sure, the slave trade would continue for decades, and Brazil would wait until near the end of the next century before abolishing it. The actual transporting of slaves from Africa reached it most frenetic pace during the twenty years following creation of the panorama as plantation agriculture developed intensively in the Western Hemisphere. But it is a landmark that every slave in Portugal received his or her freedom in 1770, as did any slave who accompanied his or her owners to Portugal. That it was done with a stroke of the pen and didn't require decades of argument in various legislatures shows the advantages that can come about when a wise leader is in charge.

The problem, of course, is that leaders are not always wise, and those who are given or who seize power can pursue wrong-headed paths. The establishment of Brasília is possibly a case in point. Kubitschek was not a despot who had acceded to power illegitimately; he was elected, unlike Brazilian leaders who preceded and followed him. But because of a particular constellation of events, which included the hubris of a coterie of leaders and intellectuals who thought they knew best, he was able to steer the Plano Pilato to realization, for good or for ill. One of the most affecting pieces of artwork on the grand esplanade that Niemeyer and Costa laid out as the center of their modernist city is a minimalist sculpture of two powerful figures. It is called *Os Candangos*, one of the names given to residents of Brasília today, but once a slightly pejorative term for the migrant workers who came from poor regions of the vast country to build the city. Like the tiny figures going about their business in the azulejo panorama of Lisbon, they are just as much a part of the Portuguese adventure as the mariners that started it all.

What happened when the people, *o povo*, in both Portugal and Brazil were faced with real despots is quite another story, one which sullied the two nations' reputations for large parts of the twentieth century, but from which some interesting lessons emerged.

CHAPTER SEVEN

Samba and *Saudade*

SAUDADE IS THE NAME given to that complex of nostalgia, regret, longing and memory that is said to mark the Portuguese soul. So many goodbyes! So many tears! And not just common people, but even the royal family.

Twenty years after Pombal left office (under a cloud, because when the king for whom he worked so hard died, the long knives of his enemies were unsheathed), the whole court packed up and moved to Brazil, taking with it gold, jewels and other treasure that the royals did not want to fall into the hands of Napoleon's forces which were advancing on Lisbon. But even before this abdication of authority, the country had been drifting. Maria I, the queen who fired Pombal as soon as she could, was certifiably insane and the fights and crises of the royal family at the time were as convoluted as the plot line of any long running Brazilian *telenovela* today.

Because she was so disturbed, Maria's eldest son was named her regent when he was still a child. By the time Napoleon set out on his grand plan to conquer Europe, Portugal found itself dependent on England for help to withstand the concerted efforts of the French. The royal party sailed from Lisbon on November 29, 1807, just a day before Napoleon's troops arrived. The British fought for nearly a year to push the French out of the city, while the Peninsular War between the British and French continued for five more years. During this time, British officials took on many of the day-to-day responsibilities of government in Portugal while the Portuguese royal family tarried in Brazil.

It took an uprising on the home front when liberal forces demanded a constitution and the return of the monarch before the king and court—Maria I died in 1816—returned to Portugal in 1821. There followed one of those family fights that are bad enough when the stakes are small but are horrendous when kingdoms are the prizes.

The João VI swore allegiance to the new Portuguese constitution, but his wife and second son Miguel refused to do so. In the crisis that followed, liberal supporters of a constitutional monarchy appeared victorious, but when the king died, all bets were off. His eldest son Pedro, who had become Emperor of Brazil, inherited the Portuguese throne, but he had no desire to come back from Brazil where he ruled a domain far larger and richer than the mother country. Instead he abdicated in favor of his seven-year-old daughter, also called Maria, on condition that his brother marry her, act as her regent and accept a liberal charter.

However Miguel, an absolutist at heart, went back on his word, renouncing the liberal charter and claiming the throne on his own behalf. Pedro, enraged by the double-cross, abdicated in Brazil in favor of his oldest son and returned to champion a more liberal approach to government in Portugal, and his daughter's claim on the Portuguese throne. The shenanigans continued for several years, involving naval battles between the two brothers' forces, with conflict that spilled over into the Azores. Finally in 1834, Miguel admitted defeat. Pedro died within a year. In the meantime Miguel's marriage to Maria was annulled and she was free to marry again.

But even when she was safely on the throne as Maria II, the rest of the century was not smooth sailing for her or for the ship of state. Well loved, she was called the Good Mother and had eleven children, dying in 1853 of complications following a miscarriage. She was succeeded as monarch by two sons in turn and then her grandson, but liberal and conservative forces continued to struggle for the country's soul.

There was one thing the two factions agreed upon: that Portugal should once again become a major force in Africa as European powers "scrambled"—that was the English term used—to divide up the continent into colonies and spheres of influence at the end of the nine-teenth century.

There is a large irony in the fact that the European country that visited sub-Saharan Africa first, that discovered the way to sail around the continent, that began the massive transport of Africans to other continents, found itself nearly left out of the "scramble." But at a time when the British were fighting the Boers for South Africa, the Belgian King Leopold was carving out his own personal kingdom in Congo, the French were consolidating their colonies on the west coast as well as in the Maghreb, and the Germans were pushing their claims in East and Central Africa, the Portuguese were having trouble claiming title to a swath across the continent from Angola to Mozambique.

Reading histories of the period written by historians from other nations, one learns little about Portugal's role in this fight. The *Mapa Cor-de-rosa*, the Rose Map, which showed the wide band where Portuguese exploration and trading posts justified Portuguese claims, was rejected by Britain, deeply marking Portuguese relations with the rest of Europe and the country's own internal fortunes. The Germans, French and Belgians didn't care what happened in that part of Africa so long as their own claims elsewhere were recognized. But Britain, egged on by imperialist entrepreneur and old Africa hand Cecil Rhodes, wanted to build a railroad from Cairo to Cape Town and control all the country through which it passed. Matters came to a head in 1890 when Britain sent an ultimatum, demanding that Portuguese military forces leave territory which is now Zimbabwe and Zambia. Enormously out-numbered, the Portuguese capitulated. The whole affair was considered a great humiliation by republican factions in Portugal. The current Portuguese national anthem was written then, with patriotic verses calling on the sons of Portugal to resist the British, *os Bretões*. Needless to say, the words have since been changed; they now call for resistance to cannons, *os canhões*, which also fits the rhyme scheme. Repercussions continued throughout the next twenty years, ending in the assassination of the king and crown prince in 1908, and the establishment of a republic in October 1910.

It is difficult today to make a careful evaluation of this First Republic, in part because the historians and archivists who might have safeguarded its stories were frequently suppressed during the Estado Novo dictatorship which followed it. Suffice to say that initially a number of broad anti-clerical measures were introduced, including the legalization of divorce. But in 1926 the temper of the times had changed, so that desire for a more conservative, stable regime led to a coup which aimed to return the country to old ways. A quiet, austere economics professor, António de Oliveira Salazar became finance minister and quickly assumed the controls of the country. His repressive regime would last for nearly fifty years. His initial stated aim was to provide stable government and to reduce the country's national debt. This he achieved through stringent fiscal controls that would cast a long shadow over Portugal's future. But, he argued, in large parts of the country poverty was evenly distributed and hence more acceptable. His government argued that low wages would attract industry that was fleeing the rising wages elsewhere in Europe. Relying on the support of the Roman Catholic Church, a large military and a well-developed system of police repression, even torture, Portugal became, more than ever, a country of *saudade*.

It was during the Salazar years that fado, the music of *saudade*, came into its own, although popular memory dates the musical form back to centuries of songs sung by Portuguese mariners sadly musing on their lives and far-away loves. But while fado—the word also means "destiny" or "fate"—appears to be ready-made to express the *saudade* of centuries, it actually arose in the nineteenth century with a strong dose of African and Brazilian input. Musicologists say that it has its roots in *lundu*, an African-inspired Brazilian dance very popular in the salons of Rio. The dance known as the *modinha* contributed also; it had made the jump across the Atlantic and become a fixture in the salons of Lisbon even earlier. In 1826, shortly after the Portuguese court returned from Rio and when cultural exchanges across the Atlantic were frequent even though the sea journey took weeks, a British visitor reported that the steel strings of the Portuguese bulb-shaped guitar "seem made for this sort of music." One guitar plays "the motivo or thema, which is a beautiful and simple species of arpeggio, whilst the other improvises the most delightful airs upon it. ... This kind of music is always of an amorous, melancholy nature; to such a degree indeed, that I have seen it draw tears on many occasions from those hearers whose hearts were at all tender". Fado itself became accepted when Maria Severa- Onofriana, the mistress of a nobleman, grew famous for her renditions of the mournful songs.

During the turbulent first decades of the twentieth century, fado found voice in singers from poor urban neighborhoods. Its popularity grew as recordings, radio and movies increased its potential audience. *A Severa* (1913), the first talking picture made in Portugal was a biography of Maria Severa, considered the first fado singer, whose black shawl became part of the fadista's uniform. Obviously there was something about the songs, filled with longing, desire and regret, that spoke to the condition of Portuguese people of all classes. In the songs "nation, lover and mother are superimposed onto one another, as ... love and longing invoke both place and person," one fado scholar says. Like *saudade* itself, they sing of the "pain of absence and the pleasure of presence through memory... (of) being in two times and two places at the same time."

Beginning in the 1930s, the Salazar government began to use fado and fadistas as part of its multi-faceted program to control the country. Singers had to register in order to perform, which meant that the impromptu, marginal artists could be suppressed. Conversely, fadistas who sang in tune with the themes that Salazar's Estado Novo favored were encouraged. Indeed, fado, *futebol* and Fatima became the three focuses of government propaganda, a Portuguese version of Roman bread and circuses. Fado was an outlet where sadness and sorrow could be expressed without being transformed into political action. *Futebol*— soccer—was a diversion through which energy and aggression were channeled in acceptable ways. The sport held out the possibility of adulation and success for the few athletes who succeeded. Fatima was

Fado singers have become cultural icons in Portugal.

closely linked with the deep Roman Catholic roots of Salazar's government. In 1917 three shepherd children had a vision of the Virgin Mary there. Pilgrimages to the site became a sign of faith among devout Portuguese Catholics while the incident has captured the imagination of people all over the world seeking contact with the miraculous.

Taken together, the three were tools to keep large sections of the Portuguese population from questioning what the Salazar government was doing on other fronts. Its policies included some ambitious public works projects, but little investment in education, sometimes violent repression of those who questioned what was going on, and the intensification of Portuguese claims in Africa. Salazar greatly admired the nationalism of Benito Mussolini, and sought a way to return to the glory of Portugal's past, as Mussolini capitalized on Italy's centuries of grand civilization.

At the same time the dictatorial regime of Getúlio Vargas in Brazil was also using music for political ends. The country was rife with regional dissension. Two states were ready to secede when Vargas took office in 1930. The emphasis was put on defining a national identity. *Futebol* was pushed to the forefront as in Portugal, but the choice of two other elements in the Vargas campaigns indicates a lot about the difference between Brazil and the mother country.

Carnaval was one. The Brazilian pre-Lenten festivities might have their roots in the ecclesiastical calendar of the Roman Catholic Church, but Carnaval in Brazil was worlds apart from the far more solemn holiday celebrated in Portugal. There has always been revelry in Lisbon, Porto and the Algarve before the beginning of Lent, yet the shadow of what follows—forty days of deprivation and penitence—has always loomed ahead. In Brazil what follows has never been as important. Each region of the country developed its own variation on the theme. All were joyous, with much singing and dancing in the streets. The Vargas regime put the emphasis on the Carnaval in Rio, but also gave financial support for Carnaval celebrations and parades elsewhere, insisting that they support some theme from Brazilian history. The samba was transformed from just one of several semi-respectable musical forms into the official music of *carnaval* and by extension, of the whole of Brazil.

How samba became a symbol of a country is an example of the way skillful propaganda can pick up themes whose roots go deep and

Portugal's Estado Novo under Antônio Oliveiro Salazar (top, second from left) began in 1926, while Brazil's Estado Novo started four years later under Getúlio Vargas (bottom). Both regimes were repressive and used music and sport to channel energy that might have gone into protest.

use them to the advantage of certain interests. At least a dozen dances had developed in Brazil since the beginning of colonization. Most, like the *lundu* and *modinha*, from which fado appears to have evolved, were strongly influenced by African music and culture introduced by slaves. *Choros, maxixes, marchas* and *serenatas* were also popular at the turn of the twentieth century. Given all these contenders, samba was perhaps the least likely candidate to become the national dance, since it came from the world of small time criminals and *favelistas*, those who lived in the rough, hillside shantytowns of Rio. At one time in fact, samba was outlawed for its unsavory associations, while a man who had calluses on his right hand that came from playing samba guitar could find himself summarily expelled from a town or thrown into jail for vagrancy. It was the music of people of mixed race, and therein lay much of its attraction for the Vargas regime.

The first samba recording was made during the First World War, and by the early 1920s the musical form had become sufficiently well known to be music that young intellectuals went out slumming to listen to. Remember that Gilberto Freyre wrote about carousing with two kings of samba, Donga and Pixinguinha, as well as classical composer Heitor Villa-Lobos and fellow intellectual Sérgio Buarque de Hollanda in 1926. Pixinguinha and his group Os Oito Batutas had already been hailed in Paris, a couple of years before African American jazzmen were toasted in the City of Light, but until the era of the Estado Nova when a few middle class *sambistas* tried to bridge the gap between the mansions and the shanties, as Freyre would put it, no one listened.

It was Freyre's ideas, though, that made the difference. Along with a national petroleum council and a national steel company, by 1933 the Vargas regime was ready to propose samba as the music for Carnaval and Carnaval as the festival for all. Carmen Miranda, who would later appear in a dozen Hollywood films, starred in a talking picture *O Voz da Carnaval*, and the municipal government of Rio, the *Prefeitura*, stepped in as official organizer and backer. The shady samba of the shanties was reborn as the exultant music of a country proud of its multiple racial origins and its "genius for miscegenation," to use Freyre's terminology.

Over the next couple of decades popular musicians performed in step with the Vargas regime's direction, as part and parcel of the Estado

(Top) The samba of Brazil and and the fado of Portugal have
their origins in music created in Brazil with strong African influences,
like this lundu dance, depicted in 1835.
(Bottom) In Brazil, the Vargas regime made Carnaval a national festival,
aimed at unifying the country.

Novo. The bands played and the samba schools danced each year, continuing after Vargas pulled away from the Fascist circle of Italy's Mussolini and Spain's Franco. Unlike Portugal, which remained officially neutral during World War II, in 1942 Brazil declared war on Japan and the Axis countries, encouraged by the United States. By the end of the war, Brazil had become home to the largest U.S. Air Force base outside the U.S. itself, while the U.S. Fourth Fleet was based in Recife. This marked a decision on the part of Brazil to take a greater role in the Western Hemisphere, and also presaged growing influence of the U.S.

The Vargas government faltered in the post-war years, as labor strife grew and the stresses and strains of post-war adjustment became apparent. Vargas himself stayed in government as a member of the legislature and was re-elected president in 1952, but in 1954 he committed suicide, overcome apparently by pressures to change the way Brazil was run. The stage was thus set for Kubitschek's election in 1956, and for another grand plan to unify the country, through the construction of Brasília. During all this time, interestingly, the popular music community, which had found the Vargas years so congenial, remained out of politics except when called upon to celebrate Carnaval. Even the musical craze which followed samba, bossa nova (the new beat), was hedonistically cool. Its foremost practitioners ended up spending much time in the U.S., as the intriguing dance rhythms gained popularity around the world.

All that changed in the 1960s. The series of elected governments ended abruptly with a military coup in 1964, followed by a coup within a coup three years later. The Vargas regime began to look almost benevolent—indeed the reputation of Vargas himself as a populist father to his people grew among a large portion of the population—when the military rulers cracked down hard on dissidents.

The 1960s were years of contestation around the world, with young people leading the struggles. They spoke out against unpopular wars (Viet Nam in the U.S. and Algeria in France), for equality between races and social classes (the Civil Rights struggle in the U.S., rights for women all over the world) and national liberation (the wave of independence movements in Africa, the rise of Quebec nationalism in Canada.) Among their tools was popular music. The folk music songs of protest in the U.S. perhaps led the way, but the iconoclastic songs like those of the Beatles in the UK and Mikis Theodorakis in Greece also gave voice to political and social concern. The musicians of Brazil were no exception, perhaps to the surprise of the military dictatorship, given the docile behavior which had characterized Brazilian music since samba had become a state tool three decades earlier.

The military government cracked down hard, sending musicians, playwrights and other malcontents to jail, some to be tortured. Others were strongly encouraged to leave the country. Among them was the son of Gilberto Freyre's old friend Sérgio Buarque de Hollanda. Chico Buarque took off for Italy and France for a year, and when he returned he played cat and mouse with the censors for years. At one point his microphone was turned off in the middle of a broadcast because he was singing words that the government did not want to hear. Some of his songs were simply prohibited. His "Fado Tropical" is particularly poignant. After the Carnation Revolution in Portugal, the end, finally, of Salazar's rule, the song became an anthem calling for the whole world to become a "Portugal," that is to take up the battle against a dictatorship and make a revolution. It is an example of the way the destinies and the culture of the mother country and her large, exuberant offspring cross and re-cross.

Great political change would only come to Brazil ten years later, but what happened in Portugal in the mid-1970s was both a demonstration of *saudade* and a tribute to the resilience of a people who were able to throw off decades of silence and stagnation without bloodshed and to rebuild toward a future that has all the challenges of world conquest, but on a smaller scale. It was to be an undertaking that in its own way was an epic that has yet to find its bard.

Of course Portugal already has an official bard. *The Lusiads* Camões wrote in the sixteenth century has been read by millions of Portuguese speakers ever since. His words float, sometimes unacknowledged, in the collective unconscious of Portuguese speakers the way Shakespeare is part of the cultural heritage of English-speakers around the world whether they know it or not. That is why a recent video montage of Camões's words and images broadcast on Radio e Televisão de Portugal is so telling. In it we hear a man read an early section of *The Lusiads* where Vasco da Gama and his crews prepare to set sail, the part where Vasco da Gama describes the leave-taking on the Praia das Lágrimas, the Shore of Sorrows.

The images in the montage are far more recent than the words. Black and white and silent, they come from newsreels and early television. In them a nation sends off its finest young men, not to explore and seek fortunes, but to subdue people who want to follow the winds of liberation that have been flowing for the decades in Africa.

The pictures are followed by images from Africa itself: the young men arrive in helicopters, march, smile at the camera, torch grass huts. And lie wounded, crying, on the point of dying for the Estado Novo, for a dream corrupted. We see the bodies, fly-specked, bloated, as rotten as the war that created them. As an embodiment of *saudade*, it has few equals. Grand traditions, memories of a marvelous adventure are superimposed on the hard facts of war, which was the result of political ideas gone wrong.

How to justify a European power's presence in Africa in the years after World War II when other colonial powers were realizing, frequently to their chagrin, that the time had come to retreat? Portugal did it by talking about destiny, by playing games with what colonies are called (they became "overseas provinces"), and, most of all, by adopting Gilberto Freyre's ideas about the special genius of the Portuguese for miscegenation and their "gift" for life in the tropics. Lusotropicalism, as Freyre called it, became the justification for sending out more Portuguese colonists to Mozambique and Angola to farm in the highlands and trade in the cities. And then, because the Portuguese settlers were seen as a slap in the face to Afro-Portuguese dreams of independence, soldiers had to be sent to protect them and to put down uprisings by the African people who had been there first.

The build-up began in the early 1960s as independence movements commenced fighting in Angola. There was ferment elsewhere in the empire. In 1961 the 3,500 man garrison in Goa surrendered to Indian forces sent to annex Goa. James Fernandes, a Goan who was among those fighting from within Goa for independence, was imprisoned by the Portuguese in the 1950s. What he wrote later in a memoir about the experience provides a window onto a world where a colonial power was being stretched beyond its means.

"Most of the soldiers were simple fellows with very little education, and very little knowledge of the world, which was surprising considering that they came from the big cities of Portugal, mainly from Lisbon and

Porto." Two of them were particularly genial and several times carried books from one prisoner to another. They also arrived one evening with coffee that they'd apparently stolen from the mess which they wanted to share with their prisoner-friends. "It was cold, watery and tasteless," Fernandes recalled. "The poor quality of their coffee roused our curiosity of the quality of their food in general. And in the course of casual conversations about their barrack life, we learned that the Portuguese common soldiers ate food which was quite poor in quality."

Fernandes also noted that when he tried to get African-Portuguese sentries to talk about politics in Africa—"as a prisoner I was eager to know the feelings of the Negroes as members of a subject race"—they seemed uninformed about what was going on there. One said about South Africa, where the screws of apartheid were being tightened, that things were "very fine" there, "You get flour, you get potatoes, you get everything." The conclusion Fernandes drew was that conditions were so bad in Mozambique for blacks that the economic and apartheid conditions in South Africa seemed better.

About ten years later when the novelist-physician António Lobos Antunes did his four years of compulsory military service in Angola things had not improved. Although he was an officer, he had trouble getting paid. In letters to his wife he wrote constantly of their financial problems because his pay hadn't arrived yet even though it was supposed to be deposited in Lisbon. Just beginning his first novel, he didn't have enough money to buy paper to write on, nor to write air letters to send home. In nearly each letter, he asked his wife to send him more or to ask his mother to send some.

Change seemed a long way off. In 1968 Salazar suffered a massive cerebral hemorrhage and was replaced by Marcello Caetano, but relatively little changed, even though Caetano was viewed by some as a moderate. The African wars continued, and to outside observers they seemed to be reaching a military point of equilibrium where they could continue indefinitely.

By then, however, more than a million Portuguese men had seen military service overseas out a population of 8.5 million, while one in four Portuguese men of military age was in the armed forces at that moment. There were 150,000 serving in Africa, with more stationed on the South Pacific island of Timor, and in Macao. The resources necessary to maintain this colonial presence were considerable, and the country did not have them.

At the beginning of the 1970s Portugal was the poorest and the most illiterate country in Western Europe, and had actually lost population because of out-migration. Thousands of Portuguese did not wait around to receive their or their sons' call-up notices to be sent to fight far, far away. They left illegally, headed for other European countries where better economic conditions beckoned as well as freedom from the draft. Or they immigrated legally. Canada was one country which sent recruiters to mainland Portugal and the Azores to sign up workers, and once the men were installed on the other side of the Atlantic, they sent for their families.

As for those Portuguese who stayed, many returned from military service with their eyes opened to other political ideas and ways of doing things, including the importance of popular education. Antunes was not the only one to send back copies of booklets—reading primers and arithmetic workbooks—taken from the rebels, produced at a time when elementary education was not being stressed in Portugal. Otelo Saraiva de Carvalho, a Mozambique-born officer who would become a leader when it came time for revolution, was much influenced by the theories of guerilla struggle he learned about when working in psychological warfare in Guinea.

Other officers in the regular armed forces felt themselves hard done by as the government tried to jury-rig a fighting force. Graduates of elite military schools got cushy administrative jobs, newly-minted officers up from the ranks were pushed ahead faster than some thought wise or fair. Initially, the band of young officers who began to think of how to overthrow the Estado Novo had many motivations, but their dissatisfaction coalesced and echoed elsewhere in society until the wave finally broke.

These men were different from the mariners, adventurers, and workers who left Portugal over past centuries in great waves rolling outward, leaving *saudade* in the backwash. Some of them had come back, of course, but they arrived as if carried by eddies, like bits of foam curling back to the shores, changed, sometimes heavy with a sprinkle of gold dust and hints of riches. Most often the wavelets of returnees had produced no grander effect than would the bursting of empty bubbles of sea foam at the water's edge. But this time there was a generation of men who had served their country overseas and had come back extremely dissatisfied with what they had seen abroad and what they saw at home.

As it happened, all signs pointed to considerable civilian dissatisfaction too. Following the spike in oil prices of 1973 when Arab states withheld petroleum in the wake of the Yom Kippur War, inflation in Portugal was running at thirty percent, the highest in Europe, and labor protests were planned for May not only by industrial workers but also office workers and civil servants. Right-wing leftovers from the Salazar days were trying to push aside the more moderate elements in the government brought in following the old dictator's death.

Then on the night between April 23 and 24, to the surprise of the outside world and much of Portugal, the Armed Forces Movement, the captains of April, struck.

Given the importance of music in the building of Portuguese (and Brazilian, for that matter) identity, and the role fado played under the Salazar regime, it's fitting that the signal for the revolt was a song played shortly after midnight on a Catholic radio station. "Grândola, Vila Morena," by dissident Jose Afonso who had grown up in Mozambique, speaks of "a land of fraternity" where on each corner is a friend, and on each face equality. Over the days that followed it was sung in the street and at meetings, as the Portuguese completed a nearly bloodless change of government. A half century of repression was swept away in a wave of joy. There was only one volley fired, coming from the Civil Guard. The rest of the armed forces and police joined with crowds of ordinary people rejoicing at the change. The coup d'état came to be called the Carnation Revolution, *A Revolução dos Cravos*, because, according to the most popular version of the story, a florist who had masses of red carnations to sell, gave one to a soldier who put it in the barrel of his rifle. Others followed suit, until carnations were everywhere.

"Grândola" is not a fado, but a rousing tune, nearer a march than a lament. That it gained the prominence it did signaled profound changes in Portugal. That it is an unsettling mixture of musical modes, starting off brightly in major followed by strong, darker minor chords, is significant. "Ambiguous" and "uncertain," one musical expert calls it. As the future appeared to some.

The call to action when the Carnation Revolution began was the playing of a song "Grândola, Vila Morena" on the radio in Lisbon. This monument in the town of Grândola commemorates the occasion.

CHAPTER EIGHT

Carmo Square, Salt Cod and Suburbs

THIRTY-FIVE YEARS AFTER the Carnation Revolution, Lisbon's Carmo Square where the Armed Forces Movement stared down the legacy of Salazar is full of tourists and students on a warm spring afternoon. The jacaranda trees are in bloom, their blossoms forming mauve clouds that shade the fountain, the benches, and the tables and chairs of the cafés located around the edges. A faint sweetness from the flowers floats in the air, attracting bees, already buzzing drunkenly on the perfume.

Banners for candidates in upcoming elections to the parliament of the European Union flutter on the lamp posts. Well-dressed young people walk by, talking on cell phones, hurrying to appointments, crossing the *calçada*, the black and white mosaic pavement which is a Portuguese trademark here in Lisbon and around the Portuguese-speaking world. No one looks down, however, at the medallion a meter wide which is set in the mosaic. It honors the heroes of Carnation Revolution which marked a watershed in Portuguese history. There are no carnations evident today, but no matter.

Spiffy looking sentries are posted outside the Guarda Republicana building where on that spring day the president took shelter. It is where negotiations took place which led to a transfer of power to an interim committee headed by a general who had written about the necessity of change. The cream-colored structure appears in impeccable repair, its plaster smooth, its arching windows glistening. The new cars parked on the other sides of the square, as well as the brightly painted walls of the buildings that edge the steep street to the north, attest to recent prosperity.

Portugal did not get to this point easily. After the spontaneous outpouring of emotion following the April 1974 uprising, months of tense negotiations among the various interests followed. If a left-wing uprising led by the military was a surprise to the United States (the Nixon government had been sure that nothing like this would happen) its success attracted the attention of the Soviets, who were always quick to expand their sphere of influence. Parts of Africa, like the Congo, had already become scenes of conflict where local armies used weapons supplied by Cold War powers. American Secretary of State Henry Kissinger had secretly promised powerful artillery to the Portuguese for use in Africa against the rebel groups, some of which were being aided by the USSR and Cuba. When it was clear that continuing the African wars was going to be extremely difficult for whatever government took power after the revolution, Soviet influence was concentrated on trying to tie Portugal as closely as possible to the Soviet bloc. But that did not succeed, and a coup attempt by extreme left-wing elements in November 1975 was unsuccessful. After many crises, democratic elections for a constituent assembly were held, and a constitution was adopted in 1976.

Since then, peaceful, multi-party elections have been held, with center-left and socialist governments walking away victors most of the time. In 1986 Portugal became part of the European Community. In 1998 on the 500th anniversary of Vasco da Gama's voyage, Lisbon was the scene of a major international fair called "The Oceans, a Heritage for the Future." In 2004 it hosted soccer's Euro Cup. Recent books about Portugal provide little more than a list of these events when they come to consider the end of the twentieth century and beginning of the twenty-first. It is almost as if the dramas of the last 700 years leave little energy to consider what happens next.

To the south of the Guarda Republicana sit the ruins of the Convento do Carmo church, one of the many buildings destroyed more than 250 years ago in the Great Earthquake. The edifice itself, originally built between 1389 and 1423, was badly damaged in the quake and its aftershocks, but it was the fire that swept through the city afterwards which effected its nearly complete destruction. The great vaulted roof fell in, leaving only pillars. During Pombal's rebuilding of the city, no agreement could be reached as to how it should be reconstructed—it was above the flat land where the greatest changes to the urban plan were undertaken—and so it remained a ghostly reminder of former glory.

The ruins of the Convento do Carmo church, one of Lisbon's buildings
destroyed more than 250 years ago in the Great Earthquake.

Sentries are posted outside the Guarda Republicana building
on Carmo Square where negotiations took place during the
Carnation Revolution.

At one time it was used to store wood, but in 1864 it was acquired by the Association of Portuguese Archeologists for a museum. The Guarda Republicana is housed in the nearby former living quarters of the Convento do Carmo monks. During the republican episode between 1910 and 1926 the museum became a depository for statuary and other art work rescued, or lifted, from churches, convents and monasteries deconsecrated during that first, ill-fated attempt to separate church and state.

This spring day sound technicians are preparing for a television broadcast of a cultural program in the evening, rolling out microphones and amplifiers, unfurling banners to serve as a set. It is a juxtaposition of times and technologies that is enough to make one's head spin. A few steps away tourists are crowded on the gangway that leads from an outdoor elevator which ascends Carmo hill from the Rossio, the heart of Pombal's reconstruction. To the east, the hilltop fortress of Castelo São Jorge dating from Moorish times looms above the Pombalite buildings on their four-square streets. To the south the sun glints off the Tagus. A few ships can be spied in the channel. The reason for choosing this site for a city are evident.

There are none of the dolphins that Camões sang about in the harbor now. The oceans today also yield far fewer fish—fish that for centuries were part of Portugal's riches, and which, while less glamorous than gold, diamonds and spices, contributed much to the well being of the people. A few months before the *Revolução dos Cravos*, the last Portuguese sailing ship arrived back from a disappointing season fishing cod off Canada's Grand Banks. It was the end of at least 550 years of men in small ships sailing across the Atlantic, and then venturing out in even smaller boats, alone, to jig for cod, some of which weighed more than the fisherman did.

In 1966 the National Film Board of Canada made a short film about one of the last of these sailing vessels, *The White Ship*. The Canadian crew left Portugal that spring, shortly before cod stocks began to decline and when only five Portuguese schooners were still doing the run. The previous season three ships had perished—one sank in mid-Atlantic, one consumed by fire, one smashed on rocks off the coast of Labrador. The crew on this survivor, the *Santa Maria Manuela*, ranged in age from a sixty-year-old who was starting his fifty-second season on the Banks, to a nineteen-year-old who was going for the first time. After sailing out of the Tagus estuary beneath the great bridge that spans the river's mouth—then called the Salazar Bridge, and now renamed the 25th of April—the ship headed across the open sea. It was a fragile-looking vessel whose deck was crowded with small rowboats which individual men would use to fish from. Lots were drawn for the dories, names were painted on them, and lines and other equipment repaired while the schooner pitched up and down on the waves, tacking her way west and north. Once on the Banks, the men did as fishermen had done for generations. They rowed out in the fog, rain or sunshine to hook fish a meter long, hauled them into the dory, and then rowed them back to the ship where they pitched them on board. The aim was to have the hold full of the split and salted *bacalhau* before the season was over. Blessings "from church and state," as the film puts it, were not enough to keep the men safe. *The White Ship* turns around the death of one fisherman and ends with the somber image of the burial on a sere

The Portuguese have fished for centuries off the country's shores and as far away as the Grand Banks of Newfoundland. Declining cod stocks led to the closure off that fishery, while restrictions are being placed on fishing closer to home. This protest in 2009 contested new regulations which put fishing and the tourist industry in conflict.

hilltop cemetery in Newfoundland where the priest recites the liturgy in English and the men mumble the responses in Portuguese.

Three years after this voyage of the *Santa Maria Manuela*, the total "harvest" of cod of the Grand Banks, reached record proportions, 810,000 tons. But the end was already in sight, since the increase was not due to any increase in the number of fish available, but to technological changes which allowed diesel-powered factory ships to scoop up more and more of the stock. It was impossible for sailing vessels like the *Santa Maria Manuela* to compete with ships vacuuming up fish, and in the process of killing the cod fishery on the Grand Banks. It would take until 1992 before the extent of the disaster was recognized and the Newfoundland cod fishery was closed indefinitely. But in 1974 the Portuguese who went down to the sea in ships already could see what was happening as it became harder and harder to fill their holds with cod they caught from small boats.

The year 1974 was also a peak year for Portuguese out-migration. For the previous ten years, Portuguese moving to France accounted for about half of all immigrants to that country, or about 80,000 a year, making Paris the second largest Portuguese city in the world. (The Portuguese presence continues: in 2009, 550,000 Portuguese citizens lived in France and 236,000 Portuguese held French citizenship). In 1974 more than 7,800 Azoreans left the Portuguese islands for Canada. The reasons were many, with economic stagnation and rejection of military conscription topping the list. The demographic effects promised to be long-lasting, as most of the migrants were young men, leaving behind young women without potential partners.

Of course, out-migration from Portugal has been in existence since the first settlers headed for Madeira and the Azores before the Portuguese had rounded the tip of Africa. Those islands also were the source of immigrants to Brazil in the eighteenth century, and in the nineteenth century their men were stalwarts wherever commercial fishing was possible. In *Moby Dick*, Melville writes of the daring Azorean whalers on American ships:

> No small number of these whaling seamen belong to the Azores, where the outbound Nantucket whalers frequently touch to augment their crews from the hardy peasants of those rocky

shores. ... How it is, there is no telling, but Islanders seem to make the best whalemen.

Whaling bases on the shores of the Pacific also drew them. In British Columbia, Portuguese Joe Silvey was a legend in late 1800s. As a teenager, he jumped ship after a whaling voyage from the island of Pico, then became a barkeeper, seine fisherman and famous story-teller. Other Portuguese fishermen settled in Hawaii, joining compatriots who had come as indentured laborers to work in the sugar cane fields. Still others made their way to California ports, looked around and stayed to work in agriculture. Many of them scrimped and saved until they could buy land. Between 1920 and 1960 about sixty-five percent of all dairy farms in California were owned by Portuguese immigrants and their families. The tuna fishing fleet, where my San Diego neighbors the Raul Fernandes family got its start, was begun and largely controlled by Portuguese immigrants, particularly from the Azores and Madeira, throughout the mid-twentieth century, until over-fishing of nearby tuna stocks in the Pacific sent the fleet to the other side of the ocean. More than a million Americans claimed Portuguese descent on the 2000 U.S. census. The highest number for a single state, 330,974, was reported in California, and the highest percentage, 9.7 percent, in Rhode Island.

In Canada, generations of Portuguese fished the Grand Banks. There is strong evidence that the Portuguese crown planned on claiming Newfoundland, since it can be construed to lie on the Portuguese side of the treaty line drawn by Pope Alexander VI to divide the world between the them and the Spanish in 1493. They left their mark in place names—"Labrador" first shows up on Portuguese maps of the early sixteenth century and apparently refers to a patent given to João Fernandes, a small landowner or "lavrador" from the Azorean island of Terceira. Other Portuguese names include Conception Bay and Cape Race, named after a cape that marks the entrance to the Tagus estuary, and which presumably would have marked the heading toward home. An early Portuguese settler in Quebec City was Pierre dit le Portugais Dasilva who arrived around 1675. (He was honored by Canada Post with a postage stamp in 2003 because his trustworthy courier service was a forerunner of the mail service). He married Jeanne Greslon-Laviolette a local girl (she was fourteen) in 1677. Together they had fifteen children, founding a family whose name in its various spellings is quite common among Francophone Quebeckers. Today there are twenty Dassylvas (the spelling used by two of Pierre's sons) in the Quebec City area.

But the Portuguese did not settle in large numbers in Canada until the 1950s. The fisherman called at St. John's, Newfoundland for supplies, or to bury the dead, but they went home to a place where the winters were warmer. In the 1950s a combination of the stagnant economy in Portugal and Canadian concerns regarding labor shortages on farms and in railroad maintenance and construction, contributed to a wave of immigration. Agents went to mainland Portugal and to the Azores, particularly São Miguel, looking for men with "hardened hands." Office workers need not apply. In 1959 volcanic eruptions on the island of Faial opened the doors wider, as both the U.S. and Canada agreed to admit residents of that island as refugees from the natural disaster. Once in Canada, the men worked hard, sent for their immediate family, and in subsequent years encouraged members of their extended families to immigrate. The result is that there are more than 40,000 people of Portuguese descent in the Montreal area, most of whom are closely tied to São Miguel. Toronto's Portuguese community is larger, more than 150,000, and somewhat more diverse, drawing from several islands of the Azores as well as Madeira and mainland Portugal. According to the 2006 partial census, some 11,220 people of Brazilian descent live in Canada.

At lunchtime on this lovely spring day in Lisbon, a stop at a small restaurant catering to people working in the neighborhood is a good idea. One located on the slopes leading up from the Baixa, the lower town, has tables set out for the noontime trade. Between noon and 2:30 p.m., the menu says, clients must order more than coffee and soft drinks. Inside, the tables are taken with men apparently from nearby renovation projects, wearing dust-covered work clothes, eating the day's specials and drinking a beer. Their choice is between a quarter roasted chicken and fried potatoes or a tuna steak served with sautéed onions, and boiled potatoes, dressed with olive oil, olives, parsley and lemon. The price is about seven euros, not including the beer. The tuna seems to be the most popular, evidence that food from the sea still is a staple, despite the depleting stocks all around the world. It tastes good, too, even better with the addition of a little hot piri-piri sauce that's provided when asked for and is more evidence of the wide reach of the Portuguese; the recipe was brought back from Africa long ago.

To walk down from the Rossio is to cut across the tourist axis. There's a trailer with a sound system, blasting recordings of fado by Amália Rodrigues, the fadista icon who died in 1999. Crowds are lined up to get into an exhibit about the *Titanic* in an exhibition space above train station which dates from the late nineteenth century, but whose architectural style attempts to recall the exuberance of buildings constructed in the great period of exploration and riches at the turn of the sixteenth century.

The Rossio square, laid out as part of Pombal's reconstruction of the city, glares in the early afternoon sunshine, the waves of its black and white mosaic undulating like the air shimmering above the hot pavement. An equestrian statute of Pedro, emperor of Brazil and King of Portugal, stands in the center, and at the north end sits a theater named in honor of his daughter, Maria II, who returned from Brazil to be queen.

At the other side, where Pombal's plan meets the edge of the oldest part of the city at the bottom of the castle hill, buildings become a little seedier. This is where the fires of the auto-de-fé burned during the Inquisition, and, fittingly, in front of the Igreja de São Domingos sit both a monument to the several thousand Jews killed in the spring of 1506 when they refused to convert, and a granite wall bearing the legend "Lisbon, city of tolerance" in a dozen languages or more. There is irony here, but also a deep desire to link up with the current of thought which led Portugal to be the first European country to abolish slavery on its soil, and to repudiate the dark side of the country's past. Pombal abolished all legal differences between Old and New Christians in 1773, something which wasn't done in Spain until 1860.

But perhaps the more interesting evidence of how Portugal today is dealing with old prejudices and misdeeds can be seen in the faces of the men lounging around in the square in front of the church, the Largo São Domingos. Most of their faces are black, and it is evident that they have come rather recently from parts of the world which the Portuguese once claimed for their own.

Explanations vary as to why this square has become a gathering place for men of African origin. One has it that the church has often had an African priest. What is clear is that since the 1970s Lisbon and Portugal have changed greatly, because of the end of the African wars.

At the time of the Carnation Revolution, in addition to a sizeable military force, Portugal had around a million civilian nationals living in Angola, Mozambique and Guinea Bissau. Some were colonial administrators and representatives of companies and their families, but others had gone to Africa to settle, to farm as Europeans of various nationalities had done in large numbers since the beginning of the twentieth century. The period of greatest Portuguese settlement coincided with the post-World War II movement of British citizens to Rhodesia.

When it became clear that the new regime in Portugal would quickly cut the restive colonies free, settlers clamored to return. By August 1975, thousands of them, frightened by rival native African factions fighting for control of their newly independent nations, had booked all the flights out of Luanda, Angola for the next several months, while on the eastern coast of the continent in Mozambique only 85,000 of the 220,000 whites remained. At that point the Portuguese government began airlifting Portuguese nationals back, and chartered two ships, one to bring people, and the other to transport their belongings. More than half a million *retornados* arrived in Portugal, including more than 300,000 from Angola and 165,000 from Mozambique, during the two years following the revolution, increasing the population of continental Portugal by five percent. Given the unsettled political and economic situation—in addition to questions about the political situation in Portugal, the world was still in shock over the 1973 petroleum crisis—they appear to have been rather quickly reintegrated. This is due, according to some researchers, to the fact that they still had strong family links in Portugal, and despite their years in Africa, retained an allegiance to the mother country. In addition, as a group the people returning were better educated than the average in Portuguese society at the time, so when Portugal began to move forward in the 1980s they were well positioned to take responsible jobs in burgeoning industry and commerce. While unemployment in Portugal rose rapidly after the revolution, running between seven and eight percent for several years, it dropped in the 1990s.

Once Portugal established a stable, progressive government and entered the European Community, the country began to welcome foreign workers into its relative prosperity. Most of these newcomers were from the former African colonies including Cape Verde and, unlike most of the *retornados*, were not white. Many workers also came from Brazil. More recently, a significant number have arrived from Eastern Europe now that countries from the former Soviet bloc have gained admission to the European Union and there are no barriers to immigration from them.

On this afternoon not quite a year after the global financial melt-down of 2008, unemployment in Portugal is back up to around eight percent, double the rate of five years ago. On the narrow streets that lead away from the square are shops catering to people who recently arrived from all over the world in search of better times, but who may be finding it harder than they expected to make a living. The twenty or so men who lean against the walls surrounding the square or sit on its steps would seem to be out of work.

Gilberto Freyre's theories about the Portuguese talent for racial mixing notwithstanding, one hears complaints today that white Portuguese discriminate against people with dark skin. Before the revolution Portugal was basically white, notes Luís Batalha in his study of Cape Verdeans in Portugal. The few immigrants who arrived earlier in the twentieth century were usually well-off. Calouste Gulbenkian, a petroleum tycoon, art collector and philanthropist of Armenian descent who settled in Lisbon in 1942, is probably the most notable example. The new wave of immigrants are quite different, and for a while, Batalha says, those from Cape Verde and Africa were preferred workers in construction and domestic service because they were viewed as hardworking, and because they frequently didn't know what they were entitled to in terms of working conditions and benefits. But with the arrival of white and frequently better educated immigrants from Eastern Europe, a latent racism is showing up, he writes. Indeed, a report of the European Commission on Racial Intolerance, while praising Portugal's laws against racial and ethnic discrimination, noted that even though immigrants from Ukraine, Moldavia and the Czech Republic don't speak Portuguese when they arrive and are of a different religion, they appear to be integrating more easily than immigrants from Portugal's former colonies who share both language and religion with continental Portuguese.

After the Carnation Revolution and the independence of the African colonies, hundreds of thousands of *retornados* came back to Portugal leading to the creation of shanties. Most of these have been replaced by new housing as the country profited from becoming a member of the European Community, but a few remain.

The Centro Commercial Colombo in suburban Lisbon, opened in 1997, is one of the largest shopping centers in Europe and bears witness to Portugal's economic, political and social transformation since the 1980s.

The bulk of immigrants do not live in the center of Lisbon. Unlike North American cities, Portuguese cities followed the European pattern of relegating poor newcomers to the farther reaches of the suburbs. In the years after the great return, shantytowns sprang up on vacant land on the edges of the city, and when social housing was constructed it was usually built in the suburbs. Anthropologist Miguel Almeida de Valle says that the center of the city now is mostly populated by three groups: the well off who can afford to live in refurbished or new apartment blocks and condos; the old and women alone who acquired their housing years ago when it was cheap; and the marginal, like the men lounging on the Largo, who cling to undeveloped corners of the center city.

Most of the encircling suburbs were built to be served by the automobile—modernist, car-centered ideas of urban planning ruled in the Salazar years, and the roads were extended after the revolution—but now many of them are served by the new Mêtro system. At the end of the Linha Amerelo (the Yellow Line) is Odivelas station, opened in 2004. The train runs above ground for part of this stretch, cutting through hills to emerge on the other side, suspended above valleys that are still undeveloped. Vineyards and orchards cover a few of the hills. The landscape this early in the year is green and inviting, very much like California's coastal hill country after the winter rains.

The Mêtro station is set on the edge of the hill. Stairs lead up to a shopping street from one entrance, but at the other, the way out is down. A multi-lane highway runs through a nearby valley, but there isn't much traffic on neighborhood streets this mid-afternoon. A plump young woman whose dark skin and tightly curling hair suggest she has African roots has set up a make-shift fruit stand with a couple of boxes and a small mechanical scale to weigh the cherries, greenish peaches and bananas she has for sale. Just beyond the entrance to the station, a road curves around. To the left small shops—a paint and hardware store, a children's shop with first communion dresses in the window, a locksmith, a bakery, among others—do business on the first floor of apartment buildings. To the right, the road leads to more multi-storied apartment buildings, reached in places by steep steps that cut from one level of housing to another. The buildings are relatively new, plastered and brightlypainted in pastel colors. The common areas are grass covered, set with trees that are maybe six or eight years old and shrubs like oleanders and bougainvillea. A school and day care complex looks down toward the Mêtro station. Laundry hangs from windows of apartment houses, the pedestrians walk on sidewalks featuring the black and white mosaic found wherever the Portuguese have gone. Across the valley, red tiles roofs and white stucco buildings indicate older neighborhoods on the other side of the main roadway. On this side farther to the north, the road passes by the apartment complexes then dips down to meet a commercial and light industrial sector.

But this is a neighborhood where the Portuguese government's efforts to provide reasonable housing for its people meets vestiges of the hard years after the revolution when the country played catch-up economically. People moving to the cities of Lisbon and Porto in search of work far outstripped the housing supply, the *retornados* from Africa needed places to live. The result was that by the late 1980s it was estimated that there were 200,000 illegally constructed dwellings in the Lisbon area. This afternoon a dark skinned woman is trudging up the hill, headed presumably for the one of the apartment buildings. She carries shopping bags in her hands and a jumbo size package of disposal diapers on her head. Behind her, in waste land over which high tension power lines pass, squatters have built two shanties from plywood, plastic tarps and discarded posts. These are called *barrocos*, the same word used for the temporary constructions Pombal allowed after the 1755 earthquake. Times are better, but obviously prosperity does not extend to everyone.

Yet a visit to Odivelas should be matched with one to another suburb at the end of another Mêtro line, Amadora Este, for example. Both stations lie beyond the central transit zone, both opened in 2004, a year of major Mêtro expansion, but there are significant differences. The Amadora Este station is set in the middle of a large park, perhaps a half a hectare in size. The trees and bushes are still small, offering not much shade on a sunny day. A long rectangular reflecting pond with jets of water leaping into the air provides refreshing sound and spray. Buses arrive and depart, serving apartment developments and housing estates where architecture and the size of individual units varies.

Amadora is a separate municipality. It was a place where people from Lisbon summered—the air and water were considered particularly good. Today the town has a population of about 172,000, making it the fourth largest city in Portugal. A large part of that growth occurred during the years following the end of the African wars, and a section of Amadora, Bairro da Cova da Moura, became one of Portugal's biggest shantytowns, as people built wherever they could on formerly agricultural lands. The *barracos* in Odivelas look almost charming in comparison to the ramshackle housing people built for themselves. But over time construction was regularized, and in the surrounding area, much more upscale housing was built. Today the people who come and go from the Amadora Este station look generally better off than those who live around Odivelas. The women leaving Mêtro station this afternoon are smartly dressed, coming home, it would seem, from work, school or shopping before the late afternoon rush hour. One jogger is puffing his way around the elaborate physical fitness circuit in the parkland which surrounds the station. In the heat of the afternoon he's the only person trying out the horizontal bars and the other apparatus at the half dozen fitness stations. The scuffed look of the jogging track suggests that it is used a lot at other times of the day, though.

Along the route are placards giving instructions on how to use the equipment and marking the distance run. Then at the end there is a big sign two meters wide and three-quarters of a meter high mounted on posts shoulder high. "*Chegada*," it says, which can be variously translated as "finish line" or "arrival."

On a hill visible over the trees sits a cluster of red-roofed buildings, that, if you squint, looks a little like those hilltop fortresses and villages that the Portuguese have built for centuries. Viewed that way, "*Chegada*" seems a particularly appropriate term: the arrival and the beginning in one glance, a long journey through history in an afternoon's wanderings, as a nation of voyagers arrives at its future.

[CHAPTER NINE]

Strong Women and Spelling

THE STORY DOES NOT END there, of course. How could it, given the tenacity of the Portuguese?

Up to this point the story of the Portuguese has been mostly a man's story. But it is time to give credit to the other half of the population. Women have been imentioned most frequently when they brought estates into a marriage or because they had strong, or weak, sons. Philippa of Lancaster was the mother of the princes who began the Age of Exploration. Inés was a martyr for love. Catarina de Bragança's dowry included Bombay and Tangier when she married Charles II of England. Maria II, empress and queen, was called the mother of the country, but was more figurehead than monarch. All were women whose prominence depended on their biological role. But the story of the Portuguese is also the story of several million other women, most lost to history, without whom the Portuguese language might be a regional dialect struggling to maintain its difference.

Let us return to that emotional scene on the shore when Vasco da Gama and his crew bid farewell to their friends and family. "Mothers, wives and sisters contributed to the chill, despairing fear that it would be many a day before any set eyes on us again, for love knows its own fear that makes it the more apprehensive," Camões has da Gama say. One of the women adds: "Husband mine, so sweet and dear to me, without whom love has willed that I should find life unbearable, what makes you go risking on the angry waves a life that belongs not to you, but to me?"

The men, of course, are not dissuaded, and there begins the long tradition of women in Portugal waiting at home while the men spread their genes and their language and sought their fortune abroad.

Until quite recently, the women left behind had few rights. During the brief progressive period at the beginning of the twentieth century, legal equality in marriage was proclaimed although women were not allowed to manage property or to vote. The Estado Nova took away even those changes. The constitution of 1933 said all were equal before the law "except for women, the differences resulting from their nature and for the good of the family." In fact, though, women played important roles in keeping the country going, and for some the absence of a husband, particularly if he was good about sending back money, meant a certain freedom. Canadian writer Anthony de Sá wrote about his Azorean grandmother whose husband spent three years in South America, that while a woman might love and miss her husband, the time he was gone meant a time without worrying about getting pregnant. In addition, while his approval might be needed to buy and sell property, when he was away the decisions were made by the wife at home, and he rubber-stamped them. The money he sent back to Portugal became an extremely important factor in the Portuguese economy: each village had its share of *casas franceses*, built by remittances sent back from France or elsewhere.

In addition, in rural Portugal, land, particularly in the north where holdings tended to be small, did not automatically go to the eldest son. Frequently the *terça*, a third of a family's holdings, was willed to one of the children, with the rest divided among the others. A daughter, married or not, could and did inherit, particularly if she was the one to stay and look after the parents in their old age.

Women also were responsible for much of the agricultural work, which gave them freedom of movement in the countryside. This was to some extent a case of necessity being the mother of invention, since for the last two centuries, at least, there were more women than men in most rural areas. The ratio in the northern district of Viana do Castelo got as low as three single men for every four single women, a sure recipe for high rate of spinsterhood. The male-female discrepancies weren't as big among married people, but by 1970 every region showed more married women than married men, indicating how many men had gone abroad to work or to fight. *Viúvas de vivos*, widows of the living, these women were frequently called, as they raised their children and kept things going while the men were away.

In recent years, it should be noted, women in Portugal and Brazil as well as elsewhere in Lusofonia have played catch-up when it comes to their rights and opportunities. The year before the Carnation Revolution, Maria Isabel Barreno, Maria Velho da Costa and Maria Teresa Horta, called unsurprisingly the Three Marias, took on Portuguese society in general and the way it treated women in particular in a best-selling book of letters, poems and meditations. They were charged with the criminal offense of writing "immoral and pornographic passages," but a marathon trial, which saw thirty writers and others intellectuals testify in their defence, ended when the prosecutor asked that the charges be revoked. His request came just three weeks before the April uprising, and in retrospect seems a foretaste of what was to come. Lídia Jorge, winner of several international literature prizes, says that the Carnation Revolution marked an enormous change in the place of women in Portuguese society. She believes that the group of women writers who have published since the mid-1970s represent an opening of spirit and style that was not possible before. Portuguese women have certainly taken their place in politics. In 2010 women accounted for nearly twenty-eight percent of Portugal's parliamentarians, a figure above the average for G8 countries, and considerably above the world-wide average of 18.4 percent. The figure was even higher in Angola, where women constituted 37 percent of parliamentarians, although Brazil lagged with only nine percent. Yet in Brazil Dilma Rousseff was hand-picked by outgoing president Luís Inacio Lula da Silva to be the ruling Workers' Party candidate for the presidency in 2010, and as this book was going to press seemed headed for victory in the October elections.

It was abroad, though, that women made the difference when it came to the survival of the Portuguese, and in the creation of an empire considerably different from those of other colonial powers. Since so few Portuguese women followed their men, the men took partners wherever they found themselves. Yet the Portuguese succeeded in making their language the mother tongue of a far-flung rainbow of people by, in effect, redefining what it meant to be Portuguese. As one scholar says, "If the homeland's population is insufficient to control a global empire, (what must be done is) mold the people in the colonies to the closest resemblance possible: Portuguese-speaking Christians who can share additional cultural traits with Europeans. By extension, to be Portuguese is then defined by language, religion and culture—not by

Brazilian President Luís Inacio Lula da Silva picked Dilma Rousseff to be his successor in 2010 elections, a measure of how far Portuguese-speaking women have come from the Estados Novos when women did not have the vote.

ancestry." No other European colonial power stressed identity with the mother country in the same way. More recently, when Brazil began attracting large numbers of immigrants during the late nineteenth and early twentieth century, a conscious decision was made to insist that Portuguese be the language of instruction in schools. German, Italian and Japanese, the mother tongues of most immigrants to Brazil, were not allowed. The strategy is not unique to the Portuguese, of course, and has been adopted in a modified fashion elsewhere. The "Melting Pot" idea that the United States officially endorsed throughout much of the twentieth century as well as recent attempts in Quebec to make French and not ethnic origin the center point of a new Quebec national-ism have their roots in the same sort of thinking.

In Africa, asserts José Curto of York University in Toronto, trans-mission of Portuguese culture succeeded thanks to women, particularly those from the local elite, who from the seventeenth century onward, insisted on asserting their attachment to Portuguese civilization. Among the musty church registers in Luanda, Angola, he has found copies of marriage contracts which note, for example, that a particular local woman, the legitimate daughter of a Portuguese official and his wife who was herself the daughter of the local elite, was to marry the son of similar union in the Luanda cathedral. This insistence on genealogy, he says, was a way for the woman and her family to assure that her children would inherit, to guarantee their place in society. By the middle of the eighteenth century, "sons of the country," the offspring of various sorts of intermarriages and unions were occupying positions of authority in Angola, dealing with the Portuguese colonizers and sometimes being sent back to Portugal to study. The result was that by the end of the eighteenth century, the free population of Luanda numbered 3,150, of whom 1,272 were administrative and military personnel who were without a doubt white—that is of direct European origin—plus 443 white civilians, 612 mulattos and 823 blacks. Curto notes that most of the "white" women counted among the civilians must really have been the offspring of mixed unions since so few European women had made the trip to Angola. They had, "thanks to favorable socio-economic circumstances, succeeded in having their skin whitened even further."

Some of these mixed-race women were forces to be reckoned with economically. Dona Ana Joaquina dos Santos e Silva, the daughter of a Portuguese father and a *mestiça* mother, is remembered as being an extremely successful trader after her husband's death, building the only three-story house in mid-nineteenth century Luanda. In terms of providing the local officials that the Portuguese relied on, these women were the ones who saw that the next generation grew up to think of themselves as part of the Portuguese empire and, with reinforcement from the Church, that Portuguese was their language.

That was abundantly clear in Brazil, too. Perhaps the most noted example is Francisca da Silva de Oliveira. Known popularly as Chica da Silva, she was born around 1735 to a Portuguese, Antônio Caetano de Sá, and his slave, Maria da Costa, whose name suggests she came directly from the slave-trading coast of Africa. Apparently a particularly lovely young woman, Chica was first sold to Sergeant Manuel Pires Sardinha, with whom she had two sons. Both eventually were educated at the University of Coimbra in Portugal, and the younger one, Simões, became a highly placed official in the Roman Catholic Church.

Chica herself was briefly the slave of a priest but then she was acquired by a trader and diamond mine owner João Fernandes de Oliveira. They never married, but he freed her and together they had thirteen children over twenty-five years. When he returned to Portugal in order to settle his father's estate, he took their four sons who eventually received titles of nobility. The daughters remained in Brazil, where they were educated at a well regarded convent school and apparently married well. Chica never went to Portugal but remained in Brazil where she appears to have been wealthy and powerful woman until her death in 1796. When, as a candidate for a high Church office, Simões' past was examined, his sponsors spoke of the sumptuousness of his mother's home and the way the best local society was entertained there.

This was the period when Portuguese was being confirmed as the common language of that vast country for two official reasons. First, the Marquês de Pombal wanted to solidify Portugal's claim on the territory granted to Portugal by the papal treaties dividing the world between Portugal and Spain. If Portuguese was spoken throughout Brazil, Portugal's legitimacy was confirmed. Therefore Pombal railed against the use of *lingua geral*, the pidgin that Jesuit missionaries had developed from various Amerindian languages. The conflict was part of a larger one between Pombal and the powerful religious order which led ultimately to its expulsion from Portuguese territory in 1759. Second, when Brazilians began to turn to Africa for labor, the slave population came from many ethnic groups speaking several languages. In order to have a common language for work as well as to insure that slaves couldn't plot among themselves without slave-owners knowing what was happening, Portuguese was encouraged and other languages suppressed.

But there is an unofficial reason which Gilberto Freyre in his many works says was the real explanation for the triumph of Portuguese in Brazil: the pivotal role played by those Portuguese women who did cross the ocean to the new country. As Freyre wrote in *The Mansions and the Shanties*, where Portuguese women settled "fat and slow-moving, with their knowledge of the culinary arts and the hygiene of the home, with their European and Christian manner of caring for children and the sick, there European civilization sent down its deepest roots and achieved its greatest permanence" The older he grew, the more he empha-sized the influence of Portuguese women, even though these

151

women's children were only a small part of the Brazilian nation. Their sons, the scions of the landowning class, were allowed, even encouraged, to have sexual relations with slaves whose offspring, until slavery was abolished, would become the property of the family. This meant that for generations, a woman of European stock might have many grand-children who would be slaves, and with whom she might have little or nothing to do. Yet as the member of an elite, the person who would set the tone for the family and the plantation, her ideas and the language she spoke would be the determining factor in the beliefs and culture of those who grew up in her circle, Freyre maintained.

In Portugal's Asian territories the situation differed somewhat. From the beginning Portuguese officials encouraged marriages between Indian women and Portuguese men on the Malabar Coast of India and in Goa. They did this in part to counter the great number of extra-legal relations that Portuguese sailors, who were required to be unmarried when they shipped out, got themselves into. As it happened, mixing took another twist here because women of the influential Nair caste enjoyed con-siderable freedom in choosing partners. Inheritance was through the maternal line, and, while Nair women married, their husbands spent most of their time in their own mothers' families, only coming to visit at night. If a husband arrived to find his shoes or other belongings outside the door, he knew he was being divorced, and so would not be allowed to enter his former wife's house. His rival might well be a Portu-guese mariner.

Later, when an effort was made to send out young Portuguese orphan girls of good family to marry mariners stationed in Goa, they frequently turned up their noses at the Portuguese sailors they had been intended for since they came from families of higher social standing than the men. Instead, some of them married into the local elite, further extending the Portuguese reach, but in a way the home country had not intended.

Portuguese men continued east from India, through the straits of Malacca, to the Spice Islands at the western edge of the Pacific, up to China to the outpost at Macau, and then on to Japan where Nagasaki became a center for Portuguese and Roman Catholic influence in the second half of the seventeenth century. At each stop the men had liaisons with local women or with slave women they brought with them and

Relatively few Portuguese women accompanied the soldiers and traders of the Portuguese empire. In India, some of those sent out to be wives ended up marrying into the local elite because they were of higher social class than most of the men they were intended to marry.

who remained in the Portuguese outpost. The intimate contact with Portuguese language and culture was usually reinforced by school and Church, but began in the midst of a family, however temporary. Two communities made up of the descendants of Portuguese and African slaves they brought with them in coastal Sri Lanka today speak a version of Portuguese that probably would be understood by the traders of the seventeenth century.

Even farther into the Pacific, several islands in what is now Indonesia still retain traces of Portuguese contact. Alfred Russel Wallace, the nineteenth-century naturalist who formulated a theory of evolution at the same time Charles Darwin did, travelled extensively in that part of the world during the 1850s. He observed that some islanders still used Portuguese words for handkerchief, *lenço*, and knife, *faça*, even though there were perfectly good Malay words for them used on nearby islands.

On several islands of the Indonesian archipelago Portuguese creoles were spoken until the late nineteenth century. Flores had the most complete one, which included the distinctive Portuguese words for Monday, Tuesday, Wednesday Thursday and Friday: *segunda-feira, terca-feira, quatra-feira* (*kuarta* on Flores), *quinta-feira* (*kinta*) and *sexta-feira*.

And the influence continues. Standard Indonesian, Bahasa Indonesia, a language systematized from several related languages after the independence of the island nation in the 1960s, has more than a hundred words for ordinary objects that are direct borrowings from Portuguese. These include the word for fork (*garfo* in Portuguese and *garpu* in Indonesian) window (*janela* and *djendela*), cabbage (*couves* and *kubis*), and ball (*bola* and *bola*.)

Through a strange twist of fate, Portuguese actually became the language of resistance during conflict between Indonesia and the formerly Portuguese colony of East Timor in the 1970s. The small country on the eastern side of the island of Timor declared its independence after the Carnation Revolution, but hardly had a chance to start governing itself when Indonesia invaded. A bloody guerilla war was waged for more than twenty years, prompting enormous demonstrations in favor of East Timor independence in Portugal itself in 1999. The idea of a commonality of Lusaphone experience was transformed into support for a little former colony literally halfway around the world. In an irony not lost on observers, one of the first Indonesian ambassadors to Portugal when diplomatic relations between the two countries recommenced spoke perfect Portuguese. He was originally from Timor, and had served in the Portuguese army in Africa during the colonial wars there.

These linguistic markers are the more remarkable when compared to the dearth of similar traces of Dutch, even though Portuguese control of most of this area ended in the mid-1600s and the Dutch were present well into the twentieth century. The difference lies in the fact that the Dutch rulers usually brought their families with them and certainly did not have continued relations with any children they might have had illegitimately with local women.

So, as the twenty-first century unfolds, the Lusofonia—that grand community of Portuguese speakers around the world—owes everything to those women who may have spoken a local language to their children but who also passed on the language of their fathers. They are the pillars on which the future rests, because it is the Portuguese language that is the thread that binds the disparate remnants of the former empire together.

Yet despite the fact that Portuguese is spoken by so many people around the world, it is not a language with a high profile in Europe or

North America. This is nothing new. More than 100 years ago the British poet Elizabeth Barrett Browning's love poems to her husband Robert were published as *Sonnets from the Portuguese*. She did this in part because the conceit that the poems had been translated from an "obscure" language made them appear less intimate, and because few English-speakers know enough Portuguese to see through the subterfuge. Browning called her "his little Portuguese" because of her dark coloring, but that usually is forgotten. The "strangeness" of the language for English speakers continues, as Alexander McCall Smith's comic *Portuguese Irregular Verb* trilogy witnesses. The German hero passionately pursues his study of the subtleties of the language and we are expected to laugh at his efforts. A hero who studied linguistic deadends in Spanish would probably not be considered so ridiculous, and, besides, Hispanics might take offense. The Portuguese—from politeness or humility, perhaps—seem not to do so.

As for the situation in France, where so many Portuguese migrated to find work and escape the African wars, the portrayal of Manuela, the cleaning woman in Muriel Barbery's bestseller *The Elegance of the Hedgehog*, speaks volumes. She pronounces Karl Marx's last name with a "sh" at the end which, the narrator says, is "a little damp, (but) with the charm of clear skies." In other words, she is a person with many good qualities, but who is treated with condescension by even the French woman who calls her "her only friend."

Portuguese is the sixth or seventh most frequently spoken language in the world, but for various reasons Portuguese's profile is much lower than its rank. In North American universities is it usually sandwiched into a corner of Spanish or Latin American studies departments. That makes some sense for linguistic reasons since it has many points in common with Spanish and is not difficult for someone who knows another Romance language to acquire, up to a point. Anyone who can get by in Spanish or French can probably read a newspaper, or an instruction booklet in Portuguese without too much trouble.

Understanding the spoken word is something else again.

Why that is has to do with the long history of the language and the way Portuguese has elaborated on its basic legacy from Latin. What is often forgotten is that Europe was a welter of dialects that weren't quite distinct languages as recently as a couple of hundred years ago. Nearly

ORTHOGRAPHIA
DA LINGOA
PORTVGVESA.

Obra vtil, & neceſſaria, aſsi pera bem ſcreuer a lingoa
Heſpanhol, como a Latina, & quaeſquer outras,
que da Latina teem origem.

¶ Item bum tractado dos pontos das clanfulas.

Pelo Licenciado Duarte Nunez do Liaõ.

EM LISBOA,
Per Ioão de Barreira impreſſor delRei N. S.

M.D.LXXVI.

The title page of first treatise on Portuguese spelling by Duarte Nunes Leão
(1576). The Portuguese language became standardized relatively early, and
successfully resisted being taken over by Spanish even when Portugal
was controlled by Spain.

all of them had certain resemblances that linguistic historians believe, show they are related to each other through an ancestral Indo-European language (the exceptions are Hungarian, Finnish, Estonian and Basque.) But regional variations flourished, sub-groups developed, and political winds sometimes swept a particular language to power. Portugal became an independent kingdom in 1143, and the Portuguese language was adopted by the court, the law and the poets by 1296. As the Portuguese repulsed the Moors over the next 150 years, the language incorporated dialects along with the lands re-conquered. The decisive battles against the forces of what is now Spain solidified both the country and its language. By the time the Age of Exploration began it was clearly a separate language. One of the comments made about the New Christian physician and botanist Garcia da Orta is that his manuscripts indicate he probably was raised in Spanish territory, not Portuguese, because he makes mistakes in his writings that someone originally educated in Portugal would not make.

The fierce independence of the little country with great ambitions was compromised during the sixty years from 1580 to 1640 when the crown passed to Philip II of Spain and his successors. But even here Portugal was lucky because the Spanish king had been surrounded by Portuguese courtiers and spoke the language well; his mother was Isabella of Portugal, and his claim to the Portuguese crown came through her. The agreement which put him on the throne guaranteed that Portuguese would continue to be the language of law and government while he included many Portuguese nobles in his court. Thus the language was saved initially from being folded into the development of modern Spanish. When the Portuguese won back their independence after Philip's death, the language's future was secured. The documents written during that period can still be read today without much difficulty by modern Portuguese speakers.

But the language has continued to evolve, and that perhaps is part of the reason why Portuguese, despite the fact that it is spoken by more than 200 million people, falls off the radar so often. Until the mid-twentieth century Portuguese-speaking elites all over the world sent their sons to the same universities in Portugal, and the same authors were taught worldwide as examples of the best Portuguese style. Yet inexorably, in daily life the language changed, detaching itself from the written word, reflecting the world in which it was spoken. Today there frequently is a large gulf between what appears on the page and what is heard on the street.

Hoje, uma lingua que não se defende, morre, wrote Portugal's only Nobel prize winner for literature, the late José Saramago: today a language that doesn't fight, dies. It is a phrase that reverberates in other countries, as anyone who lives in French-speaking Quebec can attest. But Portuguese is the probably the only really "successful" language to be so concerned about its survival. One of the ways Portuguese speakers have begun to fight is through international cooperation for the advancement of the language. The Lusofonia, clearly taking a few tips from La Francophonie, the association of French-speaking countries, aims to bring together all countries where Portuguese speakers live to promote Portuguese language and culture around the world.

In January 2010 a world-wide spelling reform went into effect in Portugal. After more than a decade of discussion, it had already been adopted in Brazil. Less than two percent of Portuguese words are affected by the changes, so while it is perhaps a step in the right direction it is not going to make a difference to foreigners who struggle to reconcile quite different pronunciations of the same word around the world. For example, *boa tarde,* good afternoon, is a greeting that in Lisbon slips away in the sunshine when you say it, *boa tar...* with the "d" barely audible. In Brazil, though, the phrase is assertive, upbeat: *boa tardje* with the last syllable coming on like gangbusters.

One is almost tempted to see in this the difference between *saudade* and samba, a measure of the similarities and differences among peoples who share so much, but whose histories are diverging.

[CHAPTER TEN]

Sonnets from the Portuguese

A QUOTE FROM JOSE SARAMAGO is one of a dozen by Portuguese writers which are now gracing a set of granite sidewalk benches on Montreal's Boulevard St-Laurent. Beginning with a three-line love poem by Dom Diniz (1261-1325), Portugal's troubadour king, they present men and women who have written in Portuguese to the acclaim of their compatriots, and frequently the world.

The project, which includes French translations of the quotations and *azulejos* by Quebec artists inspired by the lines, was unveiled in the spring of 2009, thirty-five years after the Carnation Revolution. Funded by the City of Montreal and local groups, the elegant benches are a reminder of both the contribution of Portuguese immigrants to Montreal and the richness of Portuguese culture in general .

But if you stop to read each one as you stroll north on the busy commercial street, or better yet, have a guide who can explain why the quotes were chosen, two other things become clear. The first is that the age of Portuguese exploration and glory continues to be a dominant theme in Portuguese literature. Also, the theme of what might have been, occurs again and again.

Continuing reflection on past accomplishments, on a distant Golden Age, is understandable. Many literatures have recurring preoccupations. The American Civil War is revisited regularly by writers in the United States, for example. In 1999 Russell Banks explained why he and fellow novelist Jane Smiley came out with massive works on the Abolition movement in the U.S. at the same time: "it's our Trojan War, our myth we return to whenever we have questions about who we are."

In Portuguese literature, this tradition is pronounced. The single most important work in Portuguese literature, Camões's *The Lusiads,* was written just before the empire was to lose its way during the disastrous reign of Sebastião, and remains deeply involved in the people's vision of what and who they are.

It's not just a vision of history. In much of Portuguese literature, what might have been is frequently as important as what happened. Saramago, who is perhaps most famous for his almost allegorical *Blindness*, has written several novels which might be considered alternate history. *The History of the Siege of Lisbon* explores what would have happened if the Moorish siege of Lisbon in the thirteenth century had not been lifted with the aid of Crusaders. *The Stone Island* is a story about the whole Iberian peninsula breaking off from Europe and sailing away westward. His novel, *The Trip of the Elephant* published two years before his death in the spring of 2010, starts with a real event, the Portuguese king who sent an Indian elephant from Lisbon to Vienna overland in the 1550s, and embroiders on the incident.

Another celebrated Portuguese novel, António Lobo Antunes' *The Return of the Caravels*, mixes up voyages of exploration with the return of the Portuguese from Africa in the 1970s after the Carnation Revolution. For example, he describes the crowd of *retornados*, "ecclesiastics, astrologers from Genoa, Jewish merchants, nannies, slave traders" arriving in Lisbon where "a secretary of the King" (in 1974 Portugal hadn't had a king for more than sixty years) reviews typed lists of approved returnees, takes notes in Gothic script and then presses his ring with its royal seal on the sealing wax at the bottom of the document.

Saramago and Lobo Antunes are following the example of several novelists of the nineteenth century who peppered their fiction with twists on real events. The champion of alternate reality is the writer who many critics say was the best since Camões, Fernando Pessoa. Not only was he a wonder at imagining what might happen, he also was unsurpassed at imagining alternate personalities. In his published work he developed four different writing personas, with manuscripts written in different hands, imagined biographies, photos, styles. Not recognized when alive as a major writer, he died at forty-seven after a lifetime of working as a commercial translator and contributor to small literary journals. He left more than 25,000 pages of unpublished work, which are now in the Portuguese national archives. On the centenary of his birth in 1988 his remains were moved to the Mosteiro dos Jerónimos,

The enigmatic poet and literary critic Fernando Pessoa.

where he lies with Vasco da Gama and Camões, among other notables.

This kind of playing with reality seems be in keeping with the tradition of a nation that, long after the death of Dom Sebastião, expected him to reappear and lead the nation to new glories. Nor is it out of step with the work of another acclaimed writer of the Portuguese language, Paulo Coelho. The Brazilian, whose style and message are frequently not considered to be serious by literary critics, has enjoyed enormous popularity around the world. In his mega-best seller *The Alchemist*, the hero, a shepherd boy from Andalusia, goes off to seek his fortune and finds that the treasure he seeks is actually back home. Coelho emphasizes the duty of everyone to follow his or her own "Personal Legend," which sounds very much like the old idea of destiny, *fado*, dressed up with psychological frippery. "A Personal Legend is the path we decide to take that fills our heart with enthusiasm. It is the path of our dreams," Coelho writes. The kind of single-mindedness necessary to follow dreams successfully can be found in the life stories of many Portuguese explorers.

It is just a step away from making literary conjectures to wondering if the Portuguese and their offspring might offer an alternative vision of the world. They never claimed to be Conquistadores as the Spanish did, nor they did they slaughter populations to get spices like the Dutch, yet they controlled vast territories for centuries. They were the first Europeans to become involved in the African slave trade in a major way, yet they were also the first European country to abolish slavery at home. Both Portugal and Brazil suffered from long period of dictatorship in the twentieth century, but began the twenty-first with governments solidly based in democracy, achieved without bloody revolution. Even where things went radically wrong, as they did in Mozambique and Angola after independence, there are grounds to suspect that, had the two African countries not been considered important pawns in the Cold War and been armed by Cold War powers, the civil wars would not have lasted nearly as long as they did.

All of which leads to a bigger question: do the results of the Portuguese adventure offer hints to the rest of the world on how to proceed from here? That question has lurked beneath the surface of my interest in the Portuguese for more than ten years now and I think the answer is "yes." At this point, it seems to me that there are two areas where the Portuguese adventure resonates with the rest of the world.

1. Race and Ethnic Relations

There is no denying that Portugal has vacillated in its acceptance of "others." Although it initially welcomed refugees from the mass conversions of Jews and Muslims at the end of the fifteenth century in Spain, the New Christians were persecuted and sometimes executed in the following century, even when they fled to Portuguese colonies. Yet all these strictures were swept away at the end of the eighteenth century with a stroke of the Marquês de Pombal's pen, when slavery was abolished in Portugal and discrimination against New Christians forbidden.

Slavery persisted in Brazil for more than a hundred years after that, yet at first glance it looks as if Brazil has produced a remarkable measure of racial harmony. Certainly the situation there is very different from that found in the United States, where until recently if you had "any known blood" you were a second class citizen. There may now be a man of mixed-race heritage in the White House, but a lot of instinctive anti-black prejudice remains in the country.

The Brazilians reached their current level of inter-racial acceptance after 500 years of racial mixing, not all of it voluntary. While Gilberto Freyre wrote glowingly about the beautiful maidens that the Portuguese and their sons made pregnant, he also acknowledged that the Brazilian patriarchy in which this occurred was often brutal. For every man who legitimized his relation with an African partner there were tens of thousands who did not and who considered the mothers of their children as chattels. Today the majority of Brazilians are poor, and the darker your skin, the poorer you are likely to be.

In many respects Freyre's "racial democracy" was a hollow concept from the beginning: while racial mixing was and is one of the things Brazil should be most proud of, the country was not a democracy when he was writing his influential books. The franchise was so limited by literacy and property qualifications that only 5.7 percent of the population voted in the 1930 elections. Despite an attempt to build democracy between the Vargas dictatorship and the military coup of 1964, real democratic elections weren't held until the late 1980s.

That said, if there were one thing that could be imported from Brazil that would change the rest of the world for the better it is the idea that "race" or "color" is not an all-or-nothing affair, that racial distinctions on face value are useless. The truth is that we are complicated

Culture manifests itself in many ways—even underfoot.
These mosaics are in Lisbon, but similar *calçadas* can
be found today everywhere the Portuguese went.

amalgams of the past, and who we think our ancestors were may be quite different from reality, as the well-known Afro-American scholar Elizabeth Alexander, can attest. In the course of the PBS series *Faces of America*, she discovered that she is thirty-seven generations removed from King John of England. But does that drop of royal English blood turn her identity on its head? Not bloody likely, although for some North Americans, if the equation were the other way around, it could.

2. The Importance of Leadership.

Wanting sound leadership seems almost as banal as liking apple pie, or to use a Portuguese example, the succulent little custard tarts called *pasteis de nata*. When I first started this project and learned about what the Marquês de Pombal had accomplished, despite, or maybe because of, his authoritarian ways, the idea of the Philosopher King seemed very attractive.

But for every Pombal, Portugal and her offspring have experienced a half dozen episodes of disastrous leadership. The inbred rulers from Dom Sebastião to Maria I have demonstrated the folly of royalty marrying and intermarrying for all the wrong reasons. The dictatorships of Salazar in Portugal, and Vargas and the military in Brazil demonstrate the problems of power wielded without checks and balances. Even an ostensibly democratically elected regime like that of Juscelino Kubitschek can exercise power to the detriment of the country. Brasilia may be a modernist monument, but why was it necessary to build it? The country is now touted as one of the economic leaders of the future—it's part of the BRIC group, with Russia, India and China—but would it be further along this path, had resources gone instead into providing mundane items such as a better infrastructure for Rio and São Paulo? It's a question that requires another book to answer and somebody should write it.

The take-home lesson from this book is that good leadership is a very scarce commodity, and that if anything has been accomplished in the democratic reforms of the last 150 years it is the decline of the influence of hereditary leaders. There are corollaries and implications: be wary of the monumental, approach the big project, the grand vision with caution. The only exception might be large projects to educate the citizenry or to provide cities with sewage, water, public transportation and perhaps museums and places to make music.

What,then, should a country rely if not its leaders or its visionaries? Its people. The millions upon millions of men and women who did the best they could under the circumstances, who made love and who nurtured their children. That is the continuing legacy of the Portuguese and their descendants around the world, and they should be an inspiration to the rest of us.

Maria de Madeiros' movie *The Captains of April* documents the Carnation Revolution. She says, Portugal "can teach the world through its example, which is practically unique, of how to arrive at a real democracy by peaceful means, by humanist means."

Kenneth Maxwell, of Harvard University's David Rockefeller Center for Latin American Studies goes further. The Carnation Revolution, he says in *The Making of Portuguese Democracy*, served as an example to many countries in the years following. "In many respects the most remarkable feature of the emergence of democracy in Portugal was the triumph of the moderates," he writes. Most revolutions in the recent past had been captured by militants on the right or left, but

> the Portuguese were able to create a representative and pluralistic system of government, fully comparable to the Western European mainstream. In the context of the Portuguese revolution it was Kerensky who survived, not Lenin. It was the moderate socialist Mário Soares who eventually became president of the republic and the radical military populist (leader) ... who went first to jail and then into obscurity. In this, Portugal was the precocious forerunner of the largely peaceful transitions from authoritarianism to democracy of the late 1980s in Latin America and in Eastern Europe.

Given the violent attempts at regime change at the beginning of the twenty-first century, more than ever Portugal's example bears careful study by those who would change the world.

The example of Brazil's slow progress toward democratic, inclusive governance also offers lessons. Property and literacy qualifications kept the majority of Brazilians from qualifying as voters for much of the twentieth century. That changed, however, even before the rules were modified. Hundreds of thousands of poor Brazilians moved to large cities, learned to read because they had to in order to get work, and built their own extremely modest houses in shanty-suburbs because that was the only way to put a roof over their heads, all of which helped to qualify them as electors. Then they found a way to protest military dictatorship during sham elections of the 1970s; in 1971, twenty-one percent of ballots cast were spoiled. This sent a very clear message. At the same time, many learned to work together in community and labor organizations in order to fight against unfairness in the work place and in favor of better schools, health care and ways to safeguard the communities and housing they built with their own hands. One of the results was the election of Luiz Inacio Lula da Silva and his team of reformers. Over the last eight years Lula and friends have found that governing is harder than getting elected, but even though they have not delivered everything promised, the message that change is indeed possible is one that should be heard around the world.

Looking west toward the mouth of the Tagus River and the April 25 Bridge. Looking toward the world, the Portuguese made waves.

The Answer to the Obvious Question

OLD MR. FERNANDES has been dead for a good 25 years. The last time I was in San Diego the store that the Fernandes family had put such work and love into was closed. At some point it was divided in two, with a pizza shop or some such on one side and a liquor store on the other. When I asked people in the neighborhood they said they had no idea what had happened but they all knew about the murder of a clerk in the liquor store during an armed robbery attempt in 2004. A pretty sad way for a dream to end, it seemed to me.

So I went looking to see if I could find the three Fernandes sons, old Mr. Fernandes' grandsons. I put messages on electronic bulletin boards, I contacted the church where the Portuguese community worshipped, I called Norm Fernandes who wasn't related but who was in my graduating class at Point Loma High School. He remembered the store but had no better idea than anyone else about the fate of that branch of the Fernandeses. What Norm said, however, confirmed all the stories about the toughness of the Portuguese and their descendants. His family came from Madeira to fish off San Diego, and after serving in the U.S. Naval Reserve he fished for another two decades even though in his second season he had a ship sink under him.

But I had no luck in finding the family who sparked my fascination with things Portuguese until the summer of 2009 when I thought to contact the reference service at the San Diego Public Library. Within a couple of days, I had an address and a phone number for Raul J. Fernandes, Jr. from a recent San Diego phone book. To my surprise this new old Mr. Fernandes is now 93, still living on his own in the house he and his late wife bought in the 1950s. His sons Richard, Paul and Steve live close enough to visit frequently. Even though none of them wanted to make a career of the grocery business, Steve, who'd worked with his father until Raul Jr. retired and the store was leased out, ended up being one of the founders of Sprouts, a farmers' market-style grocery chain in California and the Southwest U.S.

A family trust owns the lot the original store stood on, and Richard, who's an architect and urban planner, has an idea of what should be the next step. The family's ties to Portugal remain close. Several times the brothers and Raul Jr. have visited Fuzeta, the coastal village near the Spanish border where Raul Sr. began fishing at the beginning of the twentieth century and to which he and his brother, like so many others, regularly sent financial help.

And it's to these roots that Richard hopes to return in developing the lot where their grocery store stood. He's had two decades of experience planning theme parks, including Euro Disney near Paris. The idea would be to combine a mix of residential and commercial uses with a first floor filled with small shops featuring different regions of Portugal and a small museum about the Portuguese in San Diego. The upper stories would be set back with the dimensions tweaked in order to play with perspective the way Disney theme parks do, so that the whole would look like a hillside village in Portugal.

It's a dream, but it's possible. They have initial city approval for the idea; there is financing to work out, and questions about parking, but he's got students and colleagues thinking about how it might be designed, he said on the phone, pride in his voice.

All right, I thought to myself after talking to him. Now that's interesting. The circle would be closed in a way. *Chegada,* as they'd say at Amadora Este; they have arrived, just as the banner declares in the suburb of Lisbon where people have succeeded in building a modern country and decent lives for themselves.

But the story, of course, is not over. The Portuguese and their offspring throughout the world are following their own "Personal Legends," to quote Paulo Coelho. They are creating their own version of reality which may be very different from anything dreamed of even 100 years ago by the founders of the first Portuguese Republic, or thirty-five years ago in the newly independent states of Africa, or ten years ago when Luís Inacio Lula da Silva's Workers' Party was fighting for great change in Brazil.

I haven't lived in San Diego since I went away to university, so perhaps this exploration should end on a cold night in the middle of the winter in Montreal where I've spent far more of my life than I did in California. The sidewalks are clear—it hasn't snowed for a week or so—but it's cold and we walk quickly. There is no question that we're a long way from Lisbon, let alone Rio, Luanda, Goa or Macau.

I've been taking Portuguese classes at the Université de Montréal. When I started this project several years ago I rather quickly picked up enough Portuguese to read newspapers and history, but speaking and understanding the spoken language escaped me. Now after five months of classes—two three-hour sessions a week—I think I've made some progress even though when I called a restaurant to make a reservation and tried to speak Portuguese the man who answered switched languages immediately.

So we enter, bringing a swirl of cold air with us into the cozy restaurant. The room which seats about forty is crowded with people enjoying a glass of dry Porto before their meal or already trying the *pasteis de bacalhau*—light little fritters made from salt cod—or something more substantial.

The maître d'hôtel greets us and I steal myself to give it a try. "*Chamamos-nos Soderstrom e tinhamos reservado para os sete horas,*" I say. It's supposed to mean "Our name is Soderstrom and we have a reservation for 7 o'clock," but I'm not sure I've got it right.

He looks at me, as if trying to determine how serious I am. "*Bem-vindos,*" he says finally, and leads us to our table. Then, after he's handed us the menus and smiled at my husband, he says to me "*Fala Sueco?*"

The "*fala*" part I realize comes from the verb *falar*, to speak, and the way the tone rises at the end of the sentence means he's asking a question. But "*Sueco*"? I haven't the foggiest. So I play for time and say in my fractured Portuguese that I speak English and French and *um pouco Português*. Ah, he says, and explains that *Sueco* is Swedish.

Of course, I should have known: it's the obvious thing to surmise from our name, even though nobody speaks Swedish in my husband's family after three generations in North America, and nobody in the family into which I was born ever did.

During the evening I try a bit more Portuguese and he is kind enough to let me struggle. But we switch languages when it comes to the important stuff, why his family came to Montreal, for example.

He was five in 1967 when they arrived from Porto for the usual reasons: more work, better education for the children, to escape "that damned war." When he says the last, he makes a gesture which my Portuguese teacher says is very rude. Everybody left then, he says, there was no future. But here... He looks around at the happy clients and smiles.

But he has memories certainly, among them those of the sea. "It can be very cruel," he says. "I know." He hesitates, as if wondering if this is the time and place to tell the story. We are strangers, guests in his restaurant, here to have a good time, and he is a man of dignity. But he decides to go on. "It was in December 1949," he says. "A winter storm. Twenty-five members of my family ... my older brother, just a baby, a month old. All of them gone, just like that." He turns away for just a second, and coughs, covering emotion that it seems he hadn't intended to express. Then he turns back to us, the perfect host again. "And now what would you like for dessert?"

Endnotes

CHAPTER 1 - SANTA MARIA
Similar surprises awaited me ... The books are *Recreating Eden: A Natural History of Botanical Gardens* (2001), *Green City: People, Nature and Urban Places* (2006) and *The Walkable City: From Haussmann's Boulevards to Jane Jacobs' Streets and Beyond* (2008), all Véhicule Press.

The road tells part of the story of how the Azores got here... "The Marine Fossils from Santa Maria Island: An Historical Overview," Patricia Madeira and others, *Açoreana*, 2007, Supl. 5: 59-73.

What was grown locally... Convicts and Orphans: Forced and State-sponsored Colonizers in the Portuguese Empire, 1550-1755 by Timothy J. Coates. Stanford: Stanford University Press, 2001.

There followed attacks by French and English corsairs... web site of Memória Portuguesa http://terrasdeportugal.wikidot.com/ilha-de-santa-maria

...in West Africa cowry shells were more important... The Egyptians and ancient Chinese also used cowries as currency: quantities have been found in tombs of the Pharaohs and there are references to using them going back to the sixteenth century BCE in China. See also http://www.britishmuseum.org/explore/highlights/highlight_objects/cm/c/cowrie_shells.aspx and ...
    http://www.billcasselman.com/unpublished_works/porcelain.htm The shells' shiny surface actually appears be the origin of the word porcelain. Marco Polo thought the finish on the elegant, delicate pottery resembled that of the shells whose name in Italian was *porcellana*, a vulgar term for female genitalia referring to fissure in the shell said to look like a vulva.

The third ship in his flotilla, the Santa Maria... "Columbus in the Azores" by Rebecca Catz. Paper delivered on April 22, 1989 at UCLA's XII Annual Symposium on Portuguese Traditions

In his log book, Columbus muses ... February 14, 1493 entry in the logs of Columbus as transcribed by Bartholomeo de las Casas in 1535. Trans. John Boyd Thacher. Found at: http://www.columbusnavigation.com/diario.shtml
.

Here on the rain shadow side ... In the early part of the twenty-first century, the Portuguese government undertook a comprehensive inventory of old buildings in the Azores. For pictures and descriptions those on Santa Maria, visit http://www.inventario.iacultura.pt/smaria/vilaporto/historia.html (in Portuguese).

The airfield was finished ...
http://www.usconsulateazores.pt/LajesField.htm#Introduction A history of the Lajes air base on Terceira which also discusses the Santa Maria installation.

Given the number of possible successors ... The following section has been inspired by several biographies. See the sources list for more complete details. But probably the best and most interesting is *Prince Henry 'the Navigator' A Life* by Peter Russell Yale University Press, New Haven and London. 2000.

Chapter 2 - Seafaring
Not only have fossils of our... A fascinating archeological web site (in Portuguese) http://www.sesimbra.com/patrimonio/g_f_brava.html

*That was about the time Muslim traders perfected...*A good mnemonic for remembering which is latitude and which longitude is to associate the latter with long lines circling the earth through the poles. Latitude lines vary in length as they mount toward the poles, being longest at the equator and only a point at a pole.

..but there is no guide as user-friendly as the North Star. The Southern Cross in the time of the Ancient Greeks was visible from the latitude of Athens, apparently, but with the movement of the earth's tilt, it disappeared below the horizon well before the Age of Exploration. When Europeans travelled south of the equator the Southern Cross was one of the discoveries.

*"The place where these islands lie ...'*Al-Farghani and the "Short Degree" by Paul Lunde. *Saudi Aramco* pages 6-17 of the May/June 1992 print edition of *Saudi Aramco World.*

*Born in 1394...*Two children were born before Duarte, Blanche who died in infancy and Afonso, who died in 1400, aged 10. Isabella came after Henrique. She was born in 1397, and was followed by another Blanche in 1398, who also died in infancy, João, 1400 and Ferdinand, 1402.

Therefore getting control of the wheat trade ...p. 10. Convicts and Orphans.

One chronicle of the period... The voyages of Cadamosto and Other Documents on Western Africa in the Second Half of the Fifteenth Century, translated and edited by G. R. Crone, London. The Hakluyt Society, Second Series, LXXX, 80, 1937 p. 8 quoted by both Beazley and Russell. The native forests were not completely destroyed on the northern part of the island.

Another reports that... Cadamosto.

The Russian term for ..."Travels in Siberia-I" by Ian Frazier, *The New Yorker*, August 3, 2009 p. 39

He shipped on at least one Portuguese ... Admiral of the Ocean Sea: A Life of Christopher Columbus, Samuel Eliot Morison, Boston: Little Brown and Company, 1942.

"The immediate effects of... The Discoverers. by Daniel J. Boorstin, Vintage Books, New York, 1985. There are many other appreciations of Vasco da Gama—several of which will be mentioned later—but Boorstin's is particularly interesting because it comes from someone who was not a scholar of the Portuguese world.

*Indeed scientists say...*Interview with U.K. Gopalan, biologist and environmentalist responsible for safeguarding some of the remaining mangroves in the region. February 2005.

CHAPTER 3 - SPICES AND SOULS
Peppercorns are berries ... http://www.plantcultures.org/plants/black_pepper_history.html. There are a couple of other peppers- that are not to be confused with chili peppers of the capsicum genus.

Trunks of palm trees held..."A Brief History: The St. Francis Church" publication of the Church of South India, no publication date or ISBN number.

He was in continual conflict... "Shipping and Spices in Asian Seas, 1500-1600" in *The Portuguese Seaborne Empire 1415-1825,* C.R. Boxer, London: Hutchinson, 1969.

How long ago the nets... p.174 *When China Ruled the Seas*

*Camões thought he was working...*Virgil and the Aeneid were Camões's points of reference, not Homer and the Iliad and Odyssey because the Greek works were much less known since they were not translated into Latin or vernacular languages until the late Renaissance.

The actual discovery... Scurvy and Vitamin C by Jason Allen Mayberry Food and Drug Law Winter 2004 http://leda.law.harvard.edu/leda/data/658/Mayberry.html

*But once seafarers stayed at sea for months...*Nearly three-quarters of the sailors who died during the Seven Years' War in British service actually died from disease, mostly from scurvy, or 133,708 out of 184,899.

Ghastly the mouth and gums... The Lusiads, translation by William Julius Mickle, 1798. There are several English translations; the prose one by William C. Atkinson is particularly easy to read.

Their strategic importance continues... See "2008 World Port Rankings" available at: "http://www.aapa-ports.org/Industry/content.cfm?ItemNumber=900, posted by the American Association of Port Authorities and http://www.eia.doe.gov/emeu/cabs/World_Oil_Transit_Chokepoints/Malacca.html posted by Energy Information Administration (EIA)

*The most flagrant case...*For more about this story see Michael Krondi's fascinating *The Taste of Conquest: The Rise and Fall of the Three Great Cities of Spice* Random House, New York 2007

*These days when people count the number...*Examples are the lists drawn up by Vistawide: http://www.vistawide.com/languages/top_30_languages.htm and Ethnologue, neither of which include Bahasa Indonesia, which is nevertheless the official language in Indonesia, a nation of 250 million people. See also "Que língua dominará o mundo" de Cristina Pombo *Expressso* 23 May 2009 p. 36

Muslim traders and mariners... It's interesting to speculate whether this example of what could be called pillow proselytizing had any effect on the way that the Portuguese treated the women they met. *The Portuguese Seaborne Empire 1415-1825.*

Since Islam was not as deeply... Portugal and the World: The Future of the Past, António Pinto da Françå and José Manuel Garcia, Lisbon: Centro Nacional de Cultura, 2002.

A Christian community is documented... Medlycott, A. (1912). "St. Thomas Christians". In *The Catholic Encyclopedia*. New York: Robert Appleton Company. Found at http://www.newadvent.org/cathen/14678a.htm

Initially he thought that Goa.. p. 138 *A History of Christianity in India: The Beginnings to 1707* By Stephen Neill, Cambridge University Press, Cambridge 1984

Among Christians, the question.. By way of example, consider that fact that the massacre of Protestants in France claimed at least 15,000 lives, while Catholics were put the sword in the Netherlands and England about the same time.
.
At the beginning the main thrust ... *All Can Be Saved: Religious Tolerance and Salvation in the Iberian Atlantic World*, Stuart B. Schwartz, New Haven: Yale University Press, 2008.

They were expelled from England... p. 108 *All Can Be Saved...* Schwartz comments that this was a period when both France and England had growing merchant classes which did not appreciate competition from the Jewish merchant class. He notes that in Eastern Europe Jews were frequently welcomed during this period by local rulers who preferred them to growing influence from a local bourgeoisie.

Garcia da Orta was... See Bombay Before the British project: http:// cham.fcsh.unl.pt/bbb/home_eng.htm

CHAPTER 4 - SLAVERY
*Peter Gomes is a name...*http://www.goacom.com/village/calangute/ See also: http://en.wikipedia.org/wiki/Angola_at_the_2006_Lusophony_Games, http://www.onlinepianoguide.com/Pianotuners/Petergomes.htm and http://www.geneall.net/P/per_page.php?id=240493

Well," Gomes told executive... A more extensive excerpt from the interview is part of the PBS series *African American Lives 2*, Section Four, "The Past is another country." Henry Louis Gates, Jr., executive producer. A study of Gomes' DNA suggests that his African ancestors probably came from Cameroon and were members of the Fulani, Tikar or Hausa tribes.

*Learned Greek slaves educated...*The Old English word for slave was quite different: þræl which is related to thrall, or one who is held in bondage. The word in Slavic languages (Rus. rab, Serbo-Croatian rob, O.C.S. rabu) are the origin of robot, something which does one's bidding.

His elite status was recognized ... See the website of the British Library exhibition on Black Europeans http://www.bl.uk/onlinegallery/features/blackeuro/ pushkinback.html

Her great-great-great... From *The Sunday Times*, June 6, 1999. "Revealed: the Queen's black ancestors", Jon Ungoed-Thomas and Eduardo Goncalves http://www.timesonline.co.uk/tol/global/article6334692.ece

Because land in much ... For an extremely detailed discussion of the Africa Europeans found, see *Africa and Africans in the Making of the Atlantic World, 1400-1800,* John Thornton, Cambridge: Cambridge University Press, 1998.

Sailors accustomed... , p. 214, *Sailing Directions (Enroute), West Coast of Europe and Northwest Coast of Africa* (Pub. 143) (Bethesda: National Geo-Spatial Intelligence Agency, 2005) s.v. "Cabo Bojador."

A slave from the higher ....Horses on the West Coast of Africa were frequently considered more valuable than humans, though.. Cadamosto reported: that "a horse and his furniture sells for from nine to fourteen negroes, according to its goodness and beauty.

The Senegal was navigable... p. 53 *A World on the Move: The Portuguese in Africa, Asia and America, 1415-1808, Relatively little settlement...* See map at Wallace G. Mills Hist. 316 5 Trade in Africa http://stmarys.ca/~wmills/course316/5Trade_Africa.html

"(What) heart, however,,,, Gomes Eanes de *Zurara* from *The Chronicle of the Discovery and Conquest of Guinea* quoted p. 242 *Prince Henry the Navigator.* by Peter Russell.

*It should be noted that the Spanish consistently....*See p. 293 of *Spain's Road to Empire: The Making of a World Power 1492-1765* by Henry Kamen, Penguin Books ,London 2003 and "Changing Attitudes: Early Spanish Immigrants in the New World" by Magnus Mörner http://www. *www-gewi.uni-graz.at/jbla/ JBLA_Band_39-2002/051_068.pdf*

*The caravels of this second...*See *L'Ancien royaume de Congo: Fondation, découverte, première évangélisation de l'ancien royaume de Congo. Règne du Grand Roi Affonso Mvemba Nzinga,* by Msgr. J. Cuvelier Desclée de Brower, Bruges, Paris, 1946 An account which draws extensively from ecclesiastical records, and which betrays certain religious biases, but which is nevertheless very interesting and informative.

The Mandingo people... See http://home.clara.net/adire/francophoneintro.htm A marvelous site for a look at current and historic West African textiles from a small gallery in London owned by Duncan Clarke, a man born in Rhodesia who also has written widely on petroleum resources in Africa

Farther north where conditions... p, 388 *Gun, Germs and Steel* by Jared Diamond, W.W. Norton, New York 1997

Africans had no need to trade with the Europeans for basic commodities.... Thornton p. 75 and 48

His letters to successive... Cuvelier p 228

That contact, however ... *1491: New Revelations of the Americas before a Person Named Columbus*, Charles C. Mann, New York: Alfred A. Knopf, 2005.

In some cases, too... The Amerindians of the North American plains would adopt the horse as soon as it was introduced by the Spaniards in the 16th century. Before then horses hadn't lived in the Western Hemisphere since at least the arrival of the first humans who crossed the Bering Sea or the Pacific (take your pick, take your migration theory) and killed almost all the big species.

It is estimated that ... *The Slave Trade: The Story of the Atlantic Slave Trade, 1440-1870*, Hugh Thomas, New York: Simon & Schuster, 1997.

One was the use of transportation... See *Convicts and Orphans*

Some New Christians were crudely expelled... *The Marrano Factory: The Portuguese Inquisition and Its New Christians, 1536-1765*, António José Saraiva, trans. H. P. Salomon and I. S. D. Sassoon, Boston: Brill, 2001.

One letter was written... My translation of *Lettres de la guerre* by António Lobo Antunes, Christian Bourgeois Editor, 2006 Paris, translated from Portuguese to French by Carlos Batista.

*Nevertheless the country boasts...*See http://www.can-angola2010.com/ Institucional/Economia/index.htm?Language=en_EN

Ribeira Grande was the name... http://www.cidadevelha.com/

CHAPTER 5 - SEX
Yet perceptive teachers saw ... *Gilberto Freyre,* Maria Lúcia G. Pallares, São Paulo: Burke Editora UNESP, 2005.

The only thing missing ... *The Mystery of Samba, Popular Music and National Identity in Brazil* by Hermano Vianna, Tr. John Charles Chasteen, Chapel Hill and London: University of North Carolina Press, 1999.

He quotes from early letters back ... It is interesting to speculate on just how much Camões had read about the Portuguese explorers to the New World. Obviously he had access to Vasco da Gama's account of his journey, and his note of thanks elsewhere to Garcia da Orta for the use of his library suggests that he may have read the early accounts also. The first 28 page letter from Brazil to Dom Manoel was written in 1500.

"We considered ourselves... Tropical Truth: A Story of Music and Revolution in Brazil, Caetano Velosa, trans. Isabel de Seno, New York: Alfred A. Knopf, 2002. *According to research...*American Journal of Human Genetics (vol 83)2008 December 83 (6) 725-6 "The genetic legacy of religious diversity and intolerance: paternal lineages of Christians, Jews, and Muslims in the Iberian Peninsula." S.M. Adams, E. Bosch, P.L. Balareque, A.C. Lee, E. Arroyo, A.M. López-Parra, M. Aler, M.S. Grifo, M. Brion, A. Corracedo, J. Lavinha, B. Martinez-Jarreeta, L. Quintana-Murci, A Picornell, M. Ramon, K. Skorecki, D.M. Behar, E. Calafell, M.A. Jobling.

*Just when the mixing occurred...*It should be noted that there was a lengthy period after the massive conversions when "purity of blood" was a factor in marriages and obtaining official posts. That meant that Jewish and Moorish ancestors were frequently hidden to avoid the sort of persecution which burst out in the 16th century and which saw Garcia da Orta's sister burned at the stake. The Jesuits also rejected descendants of converted Jews for a long period, even though at least some of the founders of the order were the grandsons of *conversos*.

As David Cleary points out... "Race, nationalism and social theory in Brazil: rethinking Gilberto Freyre" by David Cleary, a paper prepared for the David Rockefeller Center for Latin American Studies Harvard University, Cambridge, MA http://www.transcomm.ox.ac.uk/working%20papers/cleary.pdf

She was illiterate ... See *A saga da família Buarque de Hollanda: Uma Familia Brasileira*, Volume 2 By Bartolomeu Buarque de Holanda and Sônia Peçanha Casa de palavra São Paulo 2007.

In the mining country ... *Slavery and Freedom in Colonial Brazil*, A. J. R. Russell-Wood, Oxford: OneWorld Editions, 2002.

For example, more than 40 percent... p. xxvii ff *Slavery and Freedom in Colonial Brazil*.

*American slaveholders...*See http://www.monticello.org/plantation/ hemingscontro/hemings-jefferson_contro.html The official website for

Monticello, Thomas Jefferson's plantation and now a museum, archive and research center.

One of them, the Viscount of Jequintinhonha... p. 62 *Forty Years in Brazil* by Frank Bennett, 1914: http://www.archive.org/stream/fortyyearsinbraz00 bennuoft/fortyyearsinbraz00bennuoft_djvu.txt also quoted in Freyre's *Order and Progress.*

It wasn't until he had passed... Introduction to *Machado de Assis: Reflections on a Brazilian Master,* by Richard Graham University of Texas Press, Austin, 1999

They found themselves ... The *Brazilian Empire: Myths and Histories,* Emilia Viotti Da Costa, Chapel Hill: The University of North Carolina Press, 2000. This includes a very interesting comparison of the Homestead Acts in the US (and Canada had similar policies) which granted land to those who would "improve" it and the refusal by Brazilian governments to make it easy for settlers to acquire land.

Freyre roundly criticized Germans... See *As Populações Meridionais do Brasil* by Oliveira Vianna, published in 1920 and available online at: http://www.dominiopublico.gov.br/pesquisa/DetalheObraForm.do? select_action=&co_obra=19322, for a classic example of the thinking.

*When Brazilians were asked...*Data from http://wapedia.mobi/en/ Race_in_Brazil#fn_1

In part that is because the genes... Skin: a *Natural History,* Nina G. Jablonski, Berkeley: University of California Press, 2005. For an interview: http://www.npr.org/templates/story/story.php?storyId=100057939

Light skinned Europeans and Asians actually... "Scientists Cite Fastest Case of Human Evolution" : Nicolas Wade *http://www.nytimes.com/2010/07/02/ science/02tibet.html?_r=1&ref=evolution*

Today genetic studies indicate... "DNA tests probe the genomic ancestry of Brazilians." *Brazilian Journal of Medical and Biological Research* (2009) 42: 870-876 ISSN 0100-879X Review- by S.D.J. Pena1, L. Bastos Rodrigues, J.R. Pimenta1 and S.P. Bydlowski/ This review article is the fruit of more than a decade of research in Brazil and elsewhere. The basic tools used are studies of DNA sequences, particularly those on the Y chromosome (its presence means a person is male: normal females have two X chromosome, while males have an X and a Y) and of mitochondria, genetic information that is transmitted solely by women.

Musicologist Hermano.. p. 90 *The Mystery of Samba.*

In fact when democracy returned ... "The Rise and Fall of Brazilian Inequality" by Francisco H.G. Ferreira, Philippe G. Leite, and Julie A. Litchfield http://www.drclas.harvard.edu/revista/articles/view/935

Part of this victory... His exact racial profile is not clear: 70 percent of Brazilians according to one survey made at the time of his election classed him as "Pardo," but he apparently does not identify himself publicly with any racial group. It is worth noting that Fernando Henrique Cardoso, who preceded Lula as president, classified himself as "mulantinho" with "one foot in the kitchen" even though 70 percent of respondents considered him white. "Pesquisa mostra que cor de celebridades revela critérios "raciais" do Brasil" by Laura Capriglione Folha de S. Paulo November 23, 2008. http://www1.folha. uol.com.br/folha/brasil/ult96u470658.shtml

It begins "I hear the voice..." " O Outro Brasil que Vem Aí" 'Eu ouço as vozes, eu vejo as cores, eu sinto os passos, de outro Brasil que vem aí, mais tropical, mais fraternal, mais brasileiro...' My translation. Note that the play on words—'cor' means both color and race in Brazilian Portuguese—has been translated by two phrases. http://www.youtube.com/watch?v=v7-d_PbXjvMt

It offers a vision ... Bodies, Pleasures and Passions: Sexual Culture in Contemporary Brazil, Richard G. Parker, Nashville: Vanderbilt University Press, 2009.

CHAPTER 6 - CITIES AND STRONG MEN
In comparison, the Chilean quake... http://www.dw-world.de/dw/article/ 0,,5324950,00.html For a summary of the Lisbon quake's damage, see: http:/ /nisee.berkeley.edu/lisbon/

He had extensive diplomatic experience... Kenneth Maxwell's thought provoking biography *Pombal, Paradox of the Enlightenment*(Cambridge University Press 1995) is the source of much of these reflections. Also of great interest is *Une ville des Lumières: La Lisbonne de Pombal* by José-Augusto França, Bibliothèque générale de l'Ecole pratiques de hautes études VIe section. Paris, 1965

He also insisted... Interview with José Curto March 2009.

Another would be to have night soil... França, p. 79.

Only Singapore took seriously ... The terrible influence of Le Corbusier and the mid-twentieth century infatuation with the automobile to the detriment of all other forms of transportation are topics that lie at the heart of my two books about cities and the people who live in them, *Green City* and *The Walkable City.* See also *The Modernist City: An Anthropological Critique of Brasília* by James Holston, Chicago: University of Chicago Press, 1989.

One work camp was opened ... Brasília, Plan and Reality: A Study of Planned and Spontaneous Urban Development, David G. Epstein, Berkeley: University of California Press, 1973. This elaboration of a Ph.D. thesis in anthropology gives both a well-researched account of the years of construction of Brasília, as well as an evaluation of how well dreams about the city had been achieved. The author, his wife and baby lived for several months in the late 1960s in some of the middle-class housing (row houses that were part of the initial plan) and in a shack they bought (none was for rent, but Epstein explains that for $200 they were able to buy a small dwelling from a worker who wanted to go back home to Pernambuco) in one of the initially unrecognized shanty towns that sprang up around the main city construction site.

Begun to provide stability after... Note that imprisonment and even torture of political enemies was nothing new in Brazil. During the empire even José Bonifacio, now considered one of the nation's founding heroes, was hounded out of the .country.

Modernist ideas of city design ... See "The legacy of modern urbanism in Brazil Paradigm turned reality or unfinished project? by Vincente del Rio and Haroldo Gallo http://digitalcommons.calpoly.edu/crp_fac/25/

From the air and on maps ... Most recently Niemeyer (yes, in 2010 he was still alive and working) wanted to build an obelisk on the esplanade that resembled the tower of the Olympic stadium in Montreal, designed by another Modernist architect Roger Taillibert. Niemeyer's project would have been ready for 50th anniversary celebrations in April 2010, but it was shelved after much criticism from some of the leading lights of Brazil's architectural community. In the end the government decided there wasn't enough money to build it: the anniversary was marked by such events as a concert by Paul McCartney.

While some seventy percent of jobs... "Low carbon cities – Curitiba x Brasília" by Fernanda Magalhaes & Mario Duran 45th ISOCARP Congress 2009 Inter-American Development Bank http://*www.isocarp.net/Data/case_studies/1492.pdf*

To read histories of the period... A good example is *Africa Since 1800 Second edition* by Roland Oliver and Anthony Atmore, Cambridge University Press, 1972 where it isn't even mentioned. See also http://historiaaberta.com.sapo.pt/lib/doc003.htm for the ultimatum that Britain gave Portugal, and http://purl.pt/93/1/iconografia/imagens/cc976a/cc976a_3.jpg for the official Portuguese version of the Mapa cor-de-rosa from 1886. The Portuguese national anthem: http://wapedia.mobi/pt/A_Portuguesa#4

Chapter 7 - Samba and *Saudade*
It was during the Salazar years that fado... "Fado Historiography: Old Myths and new Frontiers" by Kimberly DaCosta Holton in *Portuguese Cultural Studies*, Winter 2006. Rutgers University-Newark

Its popularity grew as recordings ... The Brazilian elite sent many of their sons to Coimbra to study since the first, small law faculty in Brazil didn't open until 1828. In addition the court in Portugal and the one in Rio behaved like members of the same family, as indeed they were. For more about Maria Severa see:
http://fado.com/index.php?option=com_frontpage&Itemid=1, a website maintained by an enthusiastic group of fado fanatics with advertising support from the Portuguese music industry.

At the same time, that other Estado Novo.. See *The Mystery of Samba* for a complete development of this theme.

Most, like the lundu and modinha ..."Bresil et Portugal: Musiques d'influence multiculturelle" by Maria Inês Guimarães in Revista Redes Música 59, January-June 2007 http://*www.redesmusica.org/pdfs2/bresil.pdf*

Choros, maxixes, marchas... Choro also means tears in Portuguese, and Chico Buarque, in one of his subtle attacks on the military dictatorship of the 1960s and 1970s, played on this when he wrote a musical letter to a friend in exile. All is fine here, he sings, "Tem muito samba, muito choro e rock'n'roll" "We got a lot of samba, choro and rock n' roll." O meu caro amigo. 1975

At one time in fact, samba... "Projeto nacionalista de Getúlio Vargas se beneficiou do samba" USP Online http://www4.usp.br/index.php/educacao/1137

By the end of the war..."Brazil and World War II: The Forgotten Ally" by Frank D. McCann *Estudios Interdisiplinar de America Latina y El caribe*. Vol., No2 , July- Dec, . 1999 http://www.tau.ac.il/eial/VI_2/mccann.htm

We see the bodies, fly-specked, bloated... http://www.youtube.com/watch?v=6_xHXlPZSoI Helder Macedo. Montagem - Paulo Milhomens Música - Fernando Lopes-Graça See also: http://hlportug.wordpress.com/tag/grandes-portugueses/

Lusotropicalism, as Freyre called it... See "Mozambique: Land of The Good people ," National Geographic, August 1964 p. 197 and "Angola, Unknown Africa" September 1961, p. 347, both by Volkmar Wentzel, National Geographic

What he wrote later in a... See In Quest of Freedom by James Fernandes, Concept Publishing Company, New Delhi 1990

Otelo Saraiva, a Mozambique-born officer who ... The Making of Portuguese Democracy, Kenneth Maxwell. Cambridge: Cambridge University Press, 1995. An excellent discussion of the events leading up to the April Revolution as well as of the delicate negotiations which led to the eventual establishment of a stable government

Over the days that followed it was sung ... The song is the theme of the excellent movie about the revolution The Captains of April, by Maria de Medeiros.

"Ambiguous" and "uncertain" one musical expert calls it... Miguel Jalôta explains that the song begins in the major mode but after the first chord there is an incursion in the minor mode, which confers an ambiguous and uncertain character the music. Unsettling, in other words.

CHAPTER 8 - CARMO SQUARE, SALT COD AND SUBURBS
Henry Kissinger had secretly promised powerful... Maxwell, The Making of Portuguese Democracy. For a clear, interesting discussion of what happened after April 25, 1974, Maxwell's book has no equal. But the negotiations, foreign attempts at influence, and ideological discussions are very complicated. It is no surprise that many books about Portugal jump from 1974 to 1986 when the country joined the European Economic Community—unless you know the players, you may not be interested in the play by play.

A few months before the Revolução dos Cravo... See: http://www.marinha.pt/pt/extra/creoula/onavio/hist%C3%B3ria/pages/navio.aspx

After sailing out of the Tagus estuary...The exact timing of the Santa Maria Manuela's voyage isn't clear from the film, which seems to have been shot in two or three parts: the departure from Portugal in early April (reference is made to an ocean liner which was damaged during a storm that the Santa

Maria Manuela rode out: that must be the incident April 12, 1966 when a rogue wave killed three on the Italian ship Michelangelo); the burial in St. John's of a crewmember "smashed by a wave" later in the spring, before the trees were in leaf in Newfoundland' and the fishing itself either before or after the burial.

The Portuguese presence continues... "Double Residence": A Space for Intergenerational Relations. Portuguese Immigrants in France in the Twentieth and Twenty-First Centuries" by R. De Villanva, *Portuguese Studies Review.* 14 (2) (2006/7) 241-261 http:// *www.trentu.ca/admin/publications/psr/ 1420679.pdf*

In British Columbia, Portuguese Joe Silvey ... See: *The Remarkable Adventures of Portuguese JoeSilvey.* Madeira Park, B.C.: Habour Publishing, 2004.

Many of them scrimped and saved... http://www.loc.gov/rr/hispanic/portam/ chron3.html The Library of Congress in the US has prepared an extensive chronology of Portuguese history in that country.

They left their mark in place names ... http://www.heritage.nf.ca/exploration/ portuguese.htm. See also *Portuguese Communities in Canada,* Grace M. Anderson and David Higgs. Toronto: McClelland and Stewart, 1976.

An early settler in Quebec City... See http://acanadianfamily.com/2009/02/05/ pedro-da-silva-dit-le-portugais-premier-messager-en-nouvelle-france/

By August 1975, thousands of them... See: "Mozambique: Dismantling the Portuguese Empire" in *Time* July 7, 1975 at http://www.time.com/time/ magazine/article/0,9171,913229-4,00.html#ixzz0iirYqt64 and "Flight from Angola" *The Economist, August 16, 1975.*

*This is due, according to some researchers..."*A integração dos "retornados" no interior de Portugal: o caso do distrito da Guarda" by Nelson Clemente Santos Dias Oliveira, A paper presented at VI Congreso português da sociologia, Lisbon http://*www.aps.pt/vicongresso/pdfs/150.pdf*

In addition, as a group the people... "Race, Class, and Kin in the Negotiation of 'Internal Strangerhood' among Portuguese Retornados, 1975-2000" by Stephen C. Lubkemann, in *Europe's Invisible Migrants,* ed. Andrea L. Smith, Amsterdam University Pres, Amsterdam 2003.

*While unemployment in Portugal rose...*OECD country comparisons *http:// www.isc.temple.edu/economics/.../Wang_Abrams_ECM_graphs.pdf*

On this afternoon not quite a year ... Economic survey of Portugal 2008: Improving the functioning of the labour market: http://www.oecd.org/document/4/0,3343,en_33873108_33873764_40873604_1_1_1_1,00.html

Before the Revolution, Portugal was basically "white"... *The Cape Verdean Diaspora in Portugal: Colonial Subjects in a Postcolonial World*, Luís Batalha, Oxford: Lexington Books, 2004.

Indeed, a report of the European Commission... Comissão Europeia Contra o Racismo e a Intolerância Second Report on Portugal, 2002. http://*www.coe.int/t/dghl/monitoring/ecri/.../PRT-CbC-II-2002-033-PRT.pdf*

CHAPTER 9 - STRONG WOMEN AND SPELLING
The men, of course, are not dissuaded... *See:* Emigration and Household Structure in a Portuguese Parish, 1850-1920 by Caroline B. Brettell, *Journal of Family History*, Vol. 13, No. 1, 33-57 (1988.)

The Estado Nova took away even those changes... See: http://countrystudies.us/portugal/50.htm

In addition, in rural Portugal ... *Men Who Migrate, Women Who Wait: Population and History in a Portuguese Parish*, Caroline B. Brettell, Princeton: Princeton University Press, Princeton, 1986. An extremely readable and interesting study of one parish in Northern Portugal from the early 18th century until the 1970s. Brettell combines careful analysis of parish and other documents with observations about the differences between Portugal and other Catholic societies in Mediterranean Europe as well as Ireland and Brittany.

The year before the Carnation Revolution..."The Sexes: The Case of The Three Marias" *Time* July 23, 1973 .

In 2010 Portuguese women... "Women in National Parliaments: http://www.ipu.org/wmn-e/classif.htm

As one scholar says:... p. 177 *Convicts and Orphans* .

The result was that by the end... "'As if from a Free Womb'; Baptismal Manumissions in Conceição Parish, Luanda, 1778-1807" by José C. Curto in *Portuguese Studies Review* 10(1)(2002) 26-27

One of them Dona Ana Joaquina dos Santos e Silva ... "An Angolan Woman of Means": D. Ana Joaquina dos Santos e Silva, Mid-Nineteenth Century Luso-

African Merchant Capitalist of Luanda' by Douglas Lanthier Wheeler. Santa Barbara Portuguese Studies Review, Vol 3. p 234 1996

That was abundantly clear in Brazil, too ... Júnia Ferreira Furtado, *Chica da Silva: A Brazilian Slave in the 18th Century,* Cambridge: Cambridge University Press, 2000. It should be noted that year Freyre published his somewhat risqué memoir *O Tempo Morto e Outros Tempos* which includes reflections on the beauty of mulata women, a movie was made about Chica da Silva—called Xica da Silva—that emphasized her seductiveness, suggesting that her influence was largely sexual.

*This frequently was reinforced ...*Videos of songs from the http:// www.youtube.com/watch?v=n3ohKs4s6yE The communities are Chilaw and Batticaloa.

One of his observations... Chapter 29 , The Malay Archipelago b*y Alfred Russel Wallace http://ebooks.adelaide.edu.au/w/wallace/alfred_russel/malay/ chapter29.html*

These include the word for fork ... p. 75 ff *A Influência Poruguesa na Indonesia* by Antonio Pinto da Françâ, Tipografia Lousannese Lda Lisbon, 2003.

CHAPTER 10 - SONNETS FROM THE PORTUGUESE
The American Civil War... Blue Metropolis International Literary Festival, 1999.

For example he describes... Le Retour des Caravelles, by António Lobo Antunes Christian Bourgeois editeur, Paris, 1990, translated into French by Michelle Biudicilli and Olinda Kleiman.

"A personal legend... http://paulocoelhoblog.com/2009/06/02/your-personal-legend-2nd-of-june-2009/

They were never Conquistadores like the Spanish... See Henry Kamen, *Spain's Road to Empire: The Making of a World Power 1492-1765,* London: Penguin Books, 2003. The Spanish were far more deeply engaged in European conflicts than were the Portuguese, and Kamen suggests that influenced their strategies as they claimed new territory.

*Furthermore "racial democracy...*noted in "Race, nationalism and social theory in Brazil," by David Cleary.

The leftish government of Luís ...Leonardo Boff "Lula and the Defeat of the Casa Grande" http://www.leonardoboff.com/site-eng/vista/2006/oct27.htm

But the Gini Index... See: https://www.cia.gov/library/publications/the-world-factbook/fields/2172.html CIA World Fact Book.

And the example of Brazil's slow progress... See James Holston, *Insurgent Citizenship: Disjunctions of Democracy and Modernity in Brazil,* Princeton: Princeton University Press, 2008. The fruit of 25 years of close study of Brazilian politics and society, Holton's book begins by considering how the idea of citizenship developed in Brazil, and goes on to carefully look at the way acquiring a home profoundly changed Brazilians. While generally hopeful about the state of Brazil's governance in the early 21st century, he cautions that corruption close to Lula as well as continuing problems in the justice system (in particular its slowness) could undermine the progress made.

Sources

BOOKS OF PARTICULAR INTEREST

Ames, Glenn J. *Renascent Empire? The House of Braganza and the Quest for Stability in Portuguese Monsoon Asia, c. 1640-1683* Amsterdam: Amsterdam University Press, 2000.

Anderson, Grace M. and David Higgs. *Portuguese Communities in Canada:* Toronto: McClelland and Stewart, 1976.

Antunes, António Lobo. *Lettres de la guerre* translated from Portuguese to French by Carlos Batista, Paris: Christian Bourgeois éditeur, 2006
   Le Retour des Caravelles, translated into French by Michelle Biudicilli and Olinda Kleiman Paris: Christian Bourgeois éditeur, 1990.

Balandier, Georges. *Daily life in the Kingdom of Kongo from the 16th to the 18th century* trans. Helen Weaver, London: Allen & Unwin, 1968.

Batalha, Luís. *The Cape Verdean Diaspora in Portugal: Colonial Subjects in a Postcolonial World* Oxford: Lexington Books, 2004.

Beazley, C. Raymond. *Prince Henry the Navigator The Hero of Portugal and of Modern Discovery 1394-1460* New York: G.P. Putnam's Sons, 1894.

Bennett, Frank. *Forty Years in Brazil* 1914 http://www.archive.org/stream/fortyyearsinbraz00bennuoft/fortyyearsinbraz00bennuoft_djvu.txt

Boorstin, Daniel J. *The Discoverers* New York: Vintage Books, 1985.

Boxer, C.R. *The Portuguese Seaborne Empire 1415-1825,* London: Hutchinson of London, 1969. *Portuguese India in the Mid-Seventeenth Century.* Delhi: Oxford University Press, 1980.

Brettell, Caroline B. *Men Who Migrate, Women Who Wait: Population and History in a Portuguese Parish* Princeton: Princeton University Press, 1986.
Burnside, Madeline, *Spirits of the Passage in the 17th Century* New York: Simon & Shuster, 1997.

Calhoun, Donna Alves. *Portuguese Community of San Diego* Charleston, SC: Arcadia Publishing, 2009.

Camões, Luís Vaz de. *The Lusiads*, trans. William C. Atkinson, London: Penguin Classics, 1962

Coates, Timothy J. *Convicts and Orphans: Forced and State-sponsored Colonizers in the Portuguese Empire, 1550-1755* Stanford: Stanford University Press, 2001.

Clossey, Luke. *Salvation and Globalization in the Early Jesuit Missions* Cambridge: Cambridge University Press, 2008.

Cooper, Michael. *The Japanese Mission to Europe, 1582-1590. The Journey of Four Samurai Boys through Portugal, Spain and Italy* Folkstone UK: Global Oriental, 2005.

Crone, G. R. ed. *The voyages of Cadamosto and Other Documents on Western Africa in the Second Half of the Fifteenth Century*, London: The Hakluyt Society, Second Series, LXXX, 80, 1937.

Cuvelier, Msgr. J. *L'Ancien royaume de Congo: Fondation, découverte, première évangélisation de l'ancien royaume de Congo. Règne du Grand Roi Affonsoo Mvemba Nzinga*, Bruges, Paris: Desclée de Brower, 1946.

de Almeida, Miguel Vale. *An Earth-Colored Sea: Race, Culture and the Politics of Identity in the Post-Colonial Portuguese-Speaking World* New York: Berghahn Books, 2004.

Da Rosa, Victor Pereira and Salvato Trigo. *Azorean Emigration: A Preliminary Overview* Porto: Fernando Pessoa University Press, 1994.

Epstein, David G. *Brasília, Plan and Reality: A Study of Planned and Spontaneous Urban Development* Berkeley, University of California Press , 1973.

Fauque, Claude and Marie-Josée Thiel *Les routes de l' esclavage: Histoire d'un très grand « dérangement »* Paris: Hermé, 2004.

Fernandes, James. *In Quest of Freedom* New Delhi: Concept Publishing Company, 1990.

Françâ, António Pinto da. *A Influência Poruguesa na* Lisbon: Tipografia Lousannese Lda, 2003, and José Manuel Garcia, *Portugal and the World: The Future of the Past,* Lisbon Centro Nacional de Cultura, 2002.

França, José-Augusto. *Une ville des Lumières: La Lisbonne de Pombal* Paris: Bibliothèque générale de l'Ecole pratiques de hautes études VIe section, 1965.

Freyre, Gilberto. *The Mansions and the Shanties (Sobrados e Mucambos) The Making of Modern Brazil*. Trans. Harriet de Onís. London: Weidenfeld and Nicolson, 1963 (first published in Brazil in 1936).
The Master and the Slaves: A Study in the Development of Brazilian Civilization. Trans. Samuel Putnam. New York: Alfred Knopf 1963 (first published in Brazil in 1933)
Order and Progress Brazil from Monarchy to Republic, trans. Rod W. Horton, New York: Alfred A. Knopf, 1970 .
Tempo morto e outros tempos : trechos de um diário de adolescência e primeira mocidade, 1915-1930 Rio de Janeiro: J. Olympio, 1975.

Furtado, Júnia Ferreira. *Chica da Silva: A Brazilian Slave in the 18th Century* Cambridge: Cambridge University Press, 2000.

Gaspar, Francis X. *Leaving Pico* Hanover and London: University Press of New England, 1999.

Graham, Richard. *Machado de Assis: Reflections on a Brazilian Master* Austin: University of Texas Press, 1999.

Holston, James. *The Modernist City: An Anthropological Critique of Brasília* Chicago: University of Chicago Press, 1989.
Insurgent Citizenship: Disjunctions of Democracy and Modernity in Brazil Princeton and Oxford: Princeton University Press, 2008.

Kay, Hugh. *Salazar and Modern Portugal* New York: Hawthorn Books, 1970.

Keay, John. *The Spice Route: A History* London: John Murray, 2003.

Kurlansky, Mark. *Cod: A Biography of the Fish that Changed the World* Toronto: Vintage Canada, 1998.

Krondi, Michael. *The Taste of Conquest: The Rise and Fall of the Three Great Cities of Spice* New York: Random House, 2007.
Levathes, Louise. *When China Ruled the Seas: The Treasure Fleet of the Dragon Throne, 1405-1433*, Oxford: Oxford University Press,1994.

Lubkemann, Stephen C. "Race, Class, and Kin in the Negotiation of 'Internal Strangerhood' among Portuguese Retornados, 1975-2000" in *Europe's Invisible Migrants*, ed. Andrea L. Smith, Amsterdam: Amsterdam University Press, 2003.

Mann, Charles C. *1491: New Revelations of the Americas before a Person Named Columbus* New York: Alfred A Knopf, 2005.

Maxwell, Kenneth. *The Making of Portuguese Democracy*: Cambridge: Cambridge University Press, 1995.
  Pombal, Paradox of the Enlightenment Cambridge: Cambridge University Press, 1995.
  Naked Tropics. Essays on Empire and Other Rogues New York: Routledge, 2003.

Morison, Samuel Eliot. *Admiral of the Ocean Sea: A Life of Christopher Columbus* Boston: Little Brown and Company, 1942.

Moita, Irisalva, coordinator, *O Livro de Lisboa* Lisbon: Departamento de Intervenção Urbana de Sociedade Lisboa, 1994.

Neill, Stephen. *A History of Christianity in India: The Beginnings to 1707* Cambridge: Cambridge University Press, 1984.

Oliver, Lawrence. *Never Backward: The Autobiography of Lawrence Oliver, a Portuguese American* San Diego: Private printing, 1972.

Pallares-Burke, Maria Lúcia G. *Gilberto Freyre* São Paulo: Editora UNESP, 2005.

Parker, Richard G. *Bodies, Pleasures and Passions: Sexual Culture in Contemporary Brazil Second edition* Nashville: Vanderbilt University Press, 2009.

Russell, Peter. *Prince Henry "the Navigator": A Life* New Haven and London: Yale University Press, 2000.

Russell-Wood, A. J. R. *A World on the Move: The Portuguese in Africa, Asia, and America 1415-1808* New York: St. Martin's Press, 1992.
  Slavery and Freedom in Colonial Brazil Oxford: Oneworld Editions, 2002.

Sachs, Ignacy, Jorge Wilheim and Paulo Sérgio Pinheiro, eds. *Brazil: A Century of Change.* Chapel Hill: University of North Carolina Press, 2009 .

Saraiva, António José, trans. H. P. Salomon and I.S. D. Sassoon. *The Marrano Factory: The Portuguese Inquisition and Its New Christians 1536-1765* Boston: Brill, 2001

Schwartz, Stuart B. *All Can Be Saved: Religious Tolerance and Salvation in the Iberian Atlantic World* New Haven and London: Yale University Press, 2008

Thomas, Hugh. *The Slave Trade: The Story of the Atlantic Slave Trade 1440-1870* New York: Simon & Schuster, 1997

Thornton, John. *Africa and Africans in the Making of the Atlantic World, 1400-1800. Second Edition* Cambridge: Cambridge University Press, 1998

Velosa, Caetano, trans. Isabel de Seno. *Tropical Truth: A Story of Music and Revolution in Brazil* New York: Alfred A. Knopf, 2002

Vianna, Hermano, trans. J. C. Chasteen. *The Mystery of Samba: Popular Music and National Identity in Brazil* Chapel Hill and London: University of North Carolina Press, 1999

Viotti Da Costa, Emilia. *The Brazilian Empire: Myths and Histories* Chapel Hill and London: The University of North Carolina Press, 2000

Russel, Alfred Wallace. *The Malay Archipelago, Chapter 29* http://ebooks.adelaide.edu.au/w/wallace/alfred_russel/malay/chapter29.html

Williams, Edwin B. *From Latin to Portuguese: Historical Phonology and Morphology of the Portuguese Language* Philadelphia: University of Pennsylvania Press, 1962

Articles

Adams, S.M., E. Bosch, P.L. Balareque, et al. "The genetic legacy of religious diversity and intolerance: paternal lineages of Christians, Jews, and Muslims in the Iberian Peninsula": *American Journal of Human Genetics* 2008 December 83 (6) 725-6

Boff, Leonardo. "Lula and the Defeat of the Casa Grande" http://www.leonardoboff.com/site-eng/vista/2006/oct27.htm

Capriglione, Laura. "Pesquisa mostra que cor de celebridades revela critérios "raciais" do Brasil" *Folha de S. Paulo* November 23, 2008. http://www1.folha.uol.com.br/folha/brasil/ult96u470658.shtml

Catz, Rebecca. "Columbus in the Azores." Paper delivered on April 22, 1989 at UCLA's XII Annual Symposium on Portuguese Traditions http://www.millersville.edu/~columbus/data/spc/CATZ-04.SPK

Cleary, David. "Race, nationalism and social theory in Brazil: rethinking Gilberto Freyre," paper prepared for the David Rockefeller Center for Latin American Studies Harvard University, Cambridge, MA http:// *www.transcomm.ox.ac.uk/working%20papers/cleary.pdf*

Curto, José C. "A Resitituição de 10,000 Súbitos Ndongo "Roubados" Na Angola de Meado do Século XVII: Uma Análise Preliminar" *Actos do Colóquio Internaconal Universidade de Évora* 2002
"The Story of Nbena, 1817-20: Unlawful Enslavement and the Concept of 'Original Freedom' in Angola" *Trans-Atlantic Dimension of Ethnicity in the African Diaspora*, ed. Paul E. Lovejoy and David V. Trotman, Continuum, London and New York, 2003
"As if from a Free Womb: Baptismal Manumissions in the Conceição Parish, Luanda, 1778-1807" *Portuguese Studies Review* 10 (1) (2002) 26-57
and Raymond B. Gervais, "The Population History of Luanda during the Late Atlantic Slave Trade, 1781-1844" *African Economic History* 29 (2001) I-59

De Villanva, R. "Double Residence: A Space for Intergenerational Relations. Portuguese Immigrants in France in the Twentieth and Twenty-First Centuries" *Portuguese Studies Review*. 14 (2) (2006/7) 241-261 http:// *www.trentu.ca/admin/publications/psr/1420679.pdf*

del Rio ,Vincente and Haroldo Gallo. "The legacy of modern urbanism in Brazil. Paradigm turned reality or unfinished project?" http:// digitalcommons.calpoly.edu/crp_fac/25/

Dietze, Paul M, Damien J. Jolley, Tanya N. Chikritzhs, Susan Clemen, Paul Catalano and **Tim Stockwell** "Income inequality and alcohol attributable harm in Australia" *BMC Public Health* 2009, 9:7

Ferreira, Francisco H. G., Philippe G. Leite and Julie A. Litchfield . "The Rise and Fall of Brazilian Inequality" http://www.drclas.harvard.edu/revista/ articles/view/935

Frazier, Ian. "Travels in Siberia-I," *The New Yorker*, August 3, 2009.

Guimarães, Maria Inês. "Bresil et Portugal: Musiques d'influence multiculturelle" *Revista Redes Música 59,* January-June 2007 http:// *www.redesmusica.org/pdfs2/bresil.pdf*

Holton, Kimberly DaCosta. "Fado Historiography: Old Myths and new Frontiers" *Portuguese Cultural Studie*s, Winter 2006 Rutgers University, Newark

Hunt, Edwin S. and James M. Murray. *A History of Business in Medieval Europe 1200-1550* Cambridge: Cambridge University Press 1999.

Kozak, Jan T. and Charles D. James. *Historical Depictions of the 1755 Lisbon Earthquake* Prague: Institute of Rock Mechanics, http://nisee.berkeley.edu/lisbon/

Lunde, Paul. "Al-Farghani and the Short Degree" *Saudi Aramco* 6-17. May/June 1992.

Madeira, Patricia, Andreas Kroh, António M. de Frias Martins and Sérgio P. Ávila. "The Marine Fossils from Santa Maria Island: An Historical Overview" *Açoreana*, 2007, Supl. 5: 59.

Magalhaes, Fernanda and Mario Duran. "Low carbon cities—Curitiba x Brasília" article presented at the 45th ISOCARP Congress 2009 Inter-American Development Bank http://*www.isocarp.net/Data/case_studies/1492.pdf*

Mayberry, Jason Allen. *Scurvy and Vitamin C* Food and Drug Law Winter 2004 http://leda.law.harvard.edu/leda/data/658/Mayberry.html

McCann, Frank D. "Brazil and World War II: The Forgotten Ally" *Estudios Interdisiplinar de America Latina y El caribe.* Vol., No2 , July- Dec, . 1999 http://www.tau.ac.il/eial/VI_2/mccann.htm

Medeiros, Valério, Frederico de Holanda and Ana Paula Barros. "The Myth of the Intention: The Portuguese Urban Heritage Overseas" Proceedings of the 7th International Space Syntax Symposium http://www.sss7.org/Proceedings/05 Spatial Morphology and Urban Growth/074_Medeiros_deHolanda_Barros.pdf
Medlycott, A. "St. Thomas Christians" in *The Catholic Encyclopedia*. New York: Robert Appleton Company. Found at http://www.newadvent.org/cathen/14678a.htm

Mörner, Magnus. "Changing Attitudes: Early Spanish Immigrants in the New World" http://www. *www-gewi.uni-graz.at/jbla/JBLA_Band_39-2002/051_068.pdf*

Oliveira, Nelson Clemente Santos Dias. "A integração dos "retornados" no interior de Portugal: o caso do distrito da Guarda" Paper presented at VI Congreso português da sociologia, Lisbon http://*www.aps.pt/vicongresso/pdfs/150.pdf*

Penal, S. D. J., L. Bastos Rodrigues, J. R. Pimental and S. P. Bydlowski. "DNA tests probe the genomic ancestry of Brazil," *Brazilian Journal of Medical and Biological Research* (2009) 42: 870-876.

Ungoed-Thomas, Jon and Eduardo Goncalves. *The Sunday Times* June 6, 1999 "Revealed: the Queen's black ancestors" http://www.timesonline.co.uk/tol/global/article6334692.ece

Wentzel, Volmar. "Angola, Unknown Africa" September 1961, *National Geographic* p. 347; "Mozambique: Land of The Good People" *National Geographic* August 1964 p. 197
"A Brief History: The St. Francis Church" publication of the Church of South India, no publication date or ISBN number.

Sailing Directions (Enroute), West Coast of Europe and Northwest Coast of Africa (Pub. 143) (Bethesda: National Geo-Spatial Intelligence Agency, 2005) s.v. "Cabo Bojador."
"The Sexes: The Case of The Three Marias" *Time* July 23, 1973 http://www.time.com/time/magazine/article/0,9171,878604-2,00.html #ixzz0lVK9HjuR

Websites

Portugal history:
Archeology at http://www.sesimbra.com/patrimonio/g_f_brava.html

Cape Verde history:
http://www.cidadevelha.com/ http://whc.unesco.org/en/list/1310/gallery/

Lisbon earthquake:
http://www.dw-world.de/dw/article/0,,5324950,00.html and http://nisee.berkeley.edu/lisbon

Logs of Christopher Columbus as transcribed by Bartholmew de las Casas in 1535. Translated by John Boyd Thacher. Found at http://www.columbusnavigation.com/diario.shtml

Camões and the African wars: a montage of film and poetry:
YouTube: http://www.youtube.com/watch?v=77ZRR7BnWrk

19th century claims in Africa and their consequences: http://historiaaberta.com.sapo.pt/lib/doc003.htm for the ultimatum that Britain gave Portugal, and http://purl.pt/93/1/iconografia/imagens/cc976a/cc976a_3.jpg for the official Portuguese version of the Mapa cor-de-rosa from 1886. The Portuguese national anthem: http://wapedia.mobi/pt/A_Portuguesa#4

Fishing: http://www.marinha.pt/pt/extra/creoula/onavio/hist%C3%B3ria/pages/navio.aspx

Carnation Revolution: *Grândola, vila morena* http://www.youtube.com/watch?v=ChILI0qlTH4&feature=related

Portuguese Empire:
Extent of Portuguese as spoken language: http://www.vistawide.com/languages/top_30_languages.htm

Spice trades: http://www.plantcultures.org/plants/black_pepper_history.html

Extent of Portuguese immigration to North America: http://www.loc.gov/rr/hispanic/portam/chron3.html
http://www.heritage.nf.ca/exploration/portuguese.htm

Trading and slavery:
Black Europeans:
http://www.bl.uk/onlinegallery/features/blackeuro/pushkinback.html

Trade goods:http://www.britishmuseum.org/explore/highlights/highlight_objects/cm/c/cowrie_shells.aspx
http://www.billcasselman.com/unpublished_works/porcelain.htm

Wallace G. Mills Hist. 316 5 Trade in Africa http://stmarys.ca/~wmills/course316/5Trade_Africa.html

Thomas Jefferson: http://www.monticello.org/plantation/hemingscontro/hemings-jefferson_contro.html

Race:
Perception of race in Brazil http://wapedia.mobi/en/Race_in_Brazil#fn_1

Economics: *http://www.isc.temple.edu/economics/.../Wang_Abrams_ECM_graphs.pdf* and http://www.oecd.org/document/4/0,3343,en_33873108_3 3873764_40873604_1_1_1_1,00.html

Brazil: http://paulocoelhoblog.com/2009/06/02/your-personal-legend-2nd-of-june-2009/
https://www.cia.gov/library/publications/the-world-factbook/fields/2172.html CIA World Fact Book

Video, Music, Film

African American Lives 2, Section Four, "The Past is another country." Henry Louis Gates, Jr., executive producer

The Captains of April (Capitões de Abril), a film by Maria de Medeiros, Portugal, France, 2000. The Carnation Revolution told through the lives of several real people, as well as some invented ones

City of God (Cidade de Deus) a film by Fernando Meirelles and Katia Lund, Brazil 2002. Life in a favela of Rio de Janeiro

The Convent (O Convento) a film byManoel de Oliviera, the historic Portuguese director (born in 1907) with John Malkovich, 1995. A slow, thoughtful story about an American professor (John Malkovich) and his French wife who arrive at Portuguese convent to do research

Central Station (Central do Brasil) a film by Walter Salles, 1998. A former schoolteacher writes letters for illiterates in Rio de Janeiro's train station. She ends up accompanying a young orphaned boy home to Brazil's poor, dry Nordeste region. Tough, but with a feel-good ending.

Fados, a film by Carlos Saura A glorious musical film that delves into the roots of fado as well as showing its recent transformations.

Garapa by José Padilha, Brazil, 2009. A searing documentary about poverty in the Nordeste. "Garapa" is the Portuguese word for sugar cane juice, but which is now applied to a solution of sugar and water which is the major source of calories for many poor Brazilian families.

The White Ship, documentary about one of the last Portuguese sailing vessels that fished off the Grand Banks, National Film Board of Canada, 1966

"O Outro Brasil que Vem Aí" poem by Gilberto Freyre \http://www.youtube.com/watch?v=v7-d_PbXjvMt

Chico Buarque and Cateano Veloso sing *Calice*, their play on words with the Brazilian Portuguese "Shut Up" and religious music http://www.youtube.com/watch?v=wV4vAtPn5-Q

O Fado Tropical, Chico Buarque and Ruy Guerra http://www.youtube.com/watch?v=VHQFmBrjLCM&feature=related

Samba: Projeto nacionalista de Getúlio Vargas se beneficiou do samba" USP Online http://www4.usp.br/index.php/educacao/1137

Timeline

Some dates in the long history of the Portuguese, which goes back to Phoenician times and includes a period of several centuries as a Roman province.

711: Moorish invasion, followed by three centuries of slow reconquest of the territory which is now Portugal.

1179: Afonso I was formally recognized king of an independent Portugal.

1255: The southern region of the Algarve was added. The borders have remained more or less the same ever since.

1385: Battle of Aljubarrota when Spanish forces, aided by French troops, were turned back by the Portuguese with aid from English forces, assuring Portuguese independence from the larger kingdoms and principalities on the Iberian Peninsula. Portugal and England pledged eternal mutual aid, and an English noblewoman married the Portuguese king Dom João I.

1415: Conquest of Ceuta. João I and his sons (including Infante Henrique, Henry the Navigator) captured the rich trade center in North Africa. The beginning of the Portuguese push for empire.

1420s onward: Discovery of Atlantic Islands and expeditions down the coast of Africa. Infante Henrique encouraged voyages of discovery, trade, colonization and capture. First settlements on the Azores and Madeira islands.

1441: First slaves from Western Africa arrived in Portugal. While African slaves had been sent overland to Mediterranean ports for centuries, the first shipment of twelve Africans marks beginning of four centuries of slave trade in the Atlantic.

1480s: The Portuguese discovered the technique, *volta do mar*, as they sailed down the west coast of Africa. By allowing the ships to be carried westward by the prevailing winds from the east, they could tack south. In southern latitudes they caught the prevailing winds from the west which would carry their ships around the tip of Africa and the Cape of Good Hope.

1497-99: A small group of ships from Portugal, captained by Vasco da Gama, used *volta do mar* to enter the Indian Ocean and made their way to the west coast of India, then returned to Portugal.

1500: Pedro Alvares Cabral landed on the Brazilian coast, having allowed the *volta do mar* winds to carry his ships too far west. The landing became the basis for Portugal's claim to the riches of Brazil.

1510: The Portuguese viceroy Afonso da Albequerque captured the port of Goa, solidifying the Estado da Índia and the Portuguese trade routes which would soon extend as far as Indonesia, Japan and China.

1578-80: The young king Dom Sebasitão attempted to repeat the victories of his ancestors by invading North Africa in 1578. He disappeared in battle, and the throne passed to his uncle, a cardinal, and then to Philip I of Spain in 1580. There followed 60 years when Spain controlled Portugal.

1640: Portugal attained independence from Spain.
Through the 17th century: A royal line descending from the bastard children of João I became the rulers of Portugal, in a time when England and Holland became more aggressive in carrying out their colonial and trade ambitions. Portugal lost some of its trading power and two important bases were given away when a daughter of the new ruling house, Catarina de Bragança, married Charles II of England in 1662, bringing with her as her dowry £1 million as well as Bombay and Tangiers.

Through the 17th and 18th centuries: Following the loss of much of the India, the Portuguese turned their efforts to Brazil and to the slave trade in Africa. Religious fervor of the Inquisition led to increasing persecution of converts from Judaism and their flight from Portugal.

1775: The Great Earthquake. The Marquês de Pombal decreed sweeping changes: education was reformed, the Inquisition ended and slavery in Portugal was outlawed.

Early 19th century: Portugal was threatened by Napoleon's troops and the Portuguese court fled to Brazil, where it remained until 1821.

1825: Brazil became independent.

1889: End of slavery in Brazil.

1890: Portuguese attempts to control Africa from Mozambique to Angola rebuffed.

1910: First Portuguese Republic.

1926, 1930: Two *Estados Novos*: The conservative governments of Antônio Oliveria Salazar in Portugal (beginning in 1926) and, in Brazil, Getúlio Vargas (beginning in 1930) rule the two countries with an iron hand for decades.

Late 1950s: Brazil affirms itself: construction of Brasilia during a democratic period.

1964: A military dictatorship begins in Brazil.

1974: Carnation Revolution in Portugal, a peaceful regime change after nearly fifty years of right-wing authoritarianism, followed by an end to colonial wars and independence of colonies.

1980s: Return to democracy in Brazil.

1986: Portugal entered European Community.
1996: Lusofonia around the world: the organization of Portuguese speaking countries was formed. At the beginning of the 21st century, 223 million people around the world spoke Portuguese as an official language.

2002: A populist left-wing government was elected in 2002, and Brazil became a rising economic star as part of the BRIC group (Brazil, Russia, India and China).

Image Credits

Frontispiece licensed under Creative Commons; 27 and 42 from Woodman, Richard *The History of the Ship: The Comprehensive Story of Seafaring from the Earliest Times to the Present Day* London: The Lyons Press; 1998; 46, from Garcia da Orta *Colloquies on the Simples of Drugs.*, H. Sotheran and Co., 1913; 49 and 153 from Linschoten, Jan Huygen van *Itinerario. Voyage ofte schipvaert van naer Oost ofte Portugaels Indien, 1579-1592.* 'S-Gravenhage 1955-57; 68 Olfert Dapper from Burnside, Madeline, *Spirits of the Passage in the 17th Century* New York: Simon & Shuster 1997; 71 Jansoone, Georges; 75 Gomes, Laurentino; 79 from Freyre, Gilberto, *Tempo morto e outros tempos : trechos de um diário de adolescência e primeira mocidade, 1915-1930* J.Olympio Rio de Janeiro. 1975; 83 from Fauque, Claude and Marie-Josée Thiel *Les route de l' esclavage: Histoire d'un très grand « dérangement »* Paris: Hermé 2004; 86 Carlos Julião, Acervo da Fundação Bibliotheca Nacional; 94 from Bettencourt. José *Machado of Brazil : the life and times of Machado de Assis, Brazil's greatest novelist,* New York : C. Frank Publications, 1962; 96 *O Livro de Lisboa* Lisbon: Departamento de Intervenção Urbana de Sociedade Lisboa 1994; 102 from Maxwell, Kenneth *Pombal, Paradox of the Enlightenment* by, Cambridge: Cambridge University Press 1995; 102 from Giedion, Siegfried *Space, Time and Architecture,* Cambridge: Harvard University Press, 1959; 108 Duran Ortiz, Mario Roberto; 117 Simões, Pedro; 119, 128, and 161 Copyright Commons; 121 and 149, Agência Brasil; all photographs by Mary Soderstrom

Acknowledgements

My thanks are due to:

In Lisbon: Perry Pada, first secretary at the Embassy of Indonesia, Arif Budiman (who showed me a Lisbon I wouldn't have seen otherwise), Miguel de Vale Almeida, João Souza and his family; in Montreal: my excellent and patient Portuguese teachers, Luís Aguilar, Vitália Rodrigues de Aguilar and Alice Taveres Mascarenhas; in San Diego, the family of Raul Fernandes Jr. and Sr. particularly grandsons Steve and Richard Fernandes; in Toronto: Anthony de Sá, Jose Curto of York University, and Ricardo Sternberg and Manuela Maruja of the University of Toronto; Norman Fernandes of Waldport, OR and many other kind souls encountered in my travels. I would also like to express my gratitude to the Conseil des arts et des lettres du Québec which gave me a grant in 2000 to write *The Violets of Usamabara*. That started me traveling and led to this book, as well as three others.

Muito obrigada!

Index